Hypnosis Without Trance: How Hypnosis Really Works

By James Tripp

Acknowledgements

If I were to thank everyone who has contributed to my development as a hypnotist, I would risk near doubling the length of this book, but I do wish to thank all those directly involved in the realisation of this project: Lexi, Mum and Dad, and especially Ian Rowland for his knowledge, skills, rigour, patience and hard work in bringing this book into being.

Hypnosis Without Trance:
How Hypnosis Really Works
by James Tripp

ISBN: 978-1-8382382-0-9

Published by Real Magic Media

Contents

Introduction...8

Welcome...8
What This Book Is, and Is Not, About.............12
Who This Book Is For.......................................13
What About Therapy and Changework?.........14
Overview...16
A Note on Terminology and Grammar............17

1. Definitions and Principles.............................20

Defining Hypnosis Without Trance................20
Engagement of Beliefs....................................20
Imagination..22
Verbal and Nonverbal Communication..........24
Facilitation...25
The Alteration of Subjective Experience........26
Formal/Overt v Covert Hypnosis....................29
Formal/Overt Hypnosis...................................29
Covert Hypnosis..30
Maps and Belief Systems................................31
About Hypnotic Trance...................................37
The Hypnotic Partnership..............................42
The Ideodynamic Model.................................45
Ideomotor...47
Ideosensory..48
Ideoemotive..48
Ideocognitive..49
VAKOG..53
The Hypnotic Loop..54
Hypnotic Focus...59
Frames and Framing..61
Plausibility...65
Plausibility, Framing and 'The Big Because'....69

2. The Hypnotic Process.......................................78

The Magic Key to Learning...78
The Hypnosis Without Trance Process.........................83
Stage 1: Set-Up and Pre-Framing....................................84
Introduce Hypnosis...88
Elicit the Co-operator's Attitude...................................91
Select an Appropriate Frame..95
Stage 2: Buy-in and Focus..100
Stage 3: Managing Hypnotic Loops...............................111
Hard Tests...117
Soft Tests..117
Loop Transitioning: Expansion and Transference......124
Linking..129
Nesting..131
The Hypnotic Ladder..133
Stage 4: Loop Conclusion and Return of Control.......135
Stage 5: Credit and Empowerment...............................136

3. Suggestion (1): Verbal Patterns.....................140

Pacing and Leading..141
Direction and Suggestion...142
Direct and Indirect Suggestion.....................................144
Positive and Negative Suggestions...............................148
Presupposition...152
Subordinate Clause of Time..155
Stated or Implied 'All'..156
Awareness Predicates..157
Adverbial Presuppositions...158
Temporal Presuppositions...159
Commentary Terms...159
Linkages..162
Questions..164
Anticipation Hooks...170
Associative and Dissociative Language.........................172

Playing with Time..174
Amplifying Experience.................................176
Creating Associations in Abstract.................178
Pre-engineering Pattern...............................181
Divide and Conquer Pattern.........................185
The 'Feel That' Ambiguity.............................187

4. Suggestion (2): Nonverbal Patterns and Magic Words..192

Power Beyond Words...................................192
Analogue Marking and Embedded Commands............194
Pacing Nonverbal Messages..........................196
Shared Lucid Dreaming................................203
Pantomiming...204
Magic Words...207
Try...208
Can..209
Allow..209
Now..210
As If...212
The Present Continuous Tense......................214
Congruence in Hypnotic Communication...........215

5. Additional Catalysing Concepts.................220

The Hypnotist Leads...................................220
Flexibility and Utilisation............................225
Curiosity Framing......................................232
Contrast Convincers...................................234
Reality Reports in the Long Game..................235
Narration of Action....................................236
Managing Eye Movement.............................237
Managing Internal Dialogue..........................240
Misdirection and Overload............................242
Coaching Engagement.................................244

Final Tips...245

Laughter..245

Respect and Encouragement.................................246

Focusing..247

Now Make It Real...248

About James Tripp..251

INTRODUCTION

Introduction

Welcome

And so here you are, reading the first words of this introduction to 'Hypnosis Without Trance: How Hypnosis Really Works'. Perhaps you already know something of this work prior to the purchase of this book, but if not...

My name is James Tripp, and I am an *accidental hypnotist!*

It is 2020 as I write these words, and for over 10 years now I have travelled the globe teaching my approach to the craft of hypnosis and, whilst I have acquired an international reputation (a generally good one!), none of this was ever planned.

Reflecting back, I don't know when the *idea* of hypnosis first entered my consciousness. I'm guessing that it must have been some time during my very early childhood, probably through watching cartoon depictions of hypnosis or somesuch. Whenever it was, it was *early*, because it's been a 'thing in the world' to me for as long as I can remember. A 'thing' for sure, but certainly not one that I had directed much interest or attention towards until I hit my early 20s.

In 1991 I left school with no qualifications whatsoever and brimming with near complete contempt for what Joseph Campbell would call 'village life'. I had no qualifications simply because they seemed to be nothing more than a waste of time, given my intended career as a rock star. Playing guitar and partying just seemed a lot more relevant. Keeping this account brief: the rockstar thing didn't work out and the partying took its toll.

By the age of nineteen, it's fair to say I was 'bottoming out' in psychological terms: friends and family were worried about me and I was faced with the stark choice of going under or making the long climb to a better mind and life. I chose the latter. I'd already started to get myself together a little when my concerned mother handed me a book she had picked up from a bargain bin in a shop. It was 'The Art of Chi Gong' by Wong Kiew Kit. I have no idea why she thought I might like it (it wasn't a thing that she herself was into), but I started reading and was fascinated. The book promised that, by devoting some daily time to some simple exercises, I would develop strength, health, wellbeing and even 'psychic abilities'. What did I have to lose? I tried the first few exercises and the impact was astonishing: my mood lifted, I felt energised, and had a clarity of mind like nothing I could remember. I was instantly hooked — and so the next chapter in my life began.

It was through looking to dive deeper into this work that I encountered a local Chi Gong 'Master' who could apparently manipulate 'chi' to such a high degree that he could physically lock people up or knock them down without even touching them. I attended his class and watched him do this with his existing students over many months before he finally invited me up to 'the mat' (where all this action happened). I stood there in anticipation... and the chi manipulation began. Across the space of ten or so minutes, he locked my hands, locked me to the floor, collapsed me down, stretched me out and knocked me back flying. All without a single touch.

I will say now that this experience was *very real* and *very vivid*, and there was no conscious playing along on my part. On the face of it I could easily have taken this as *prima facie* evidence for his claims of chi manipulation, but whilst I very much wanted them to be true, I was raised by my engineer father to approach investigation with a little more critical rigour. And so I set about conducting some phenomenological experiments. Directly following my first experience, I went home to see how much of this 'chi manipulation' experience I could replicate within myself. I imagined mobilising my chi to make my arm float up, and it did just that! Just as powerfully and vividly as I had experienced at the hands of the chi gong 'master'. I also found that I could 'break the spell' by simply shifting my attention. Through my experiments, it was starting to seem that what I had experienced in the class had more to do with how I had been encouraged to move my mind and attention than with any sort of 'chi manipulation' on the part of this 'master'. This is when that old, background, cultural concept of hypnosis alighted upon my mind in the form of a question: had I actually just been 'hypnotised'?

In the spirit of genuine and open curiosity, I asked the 'master' this very question. His reply: "Hypnosis is manipulation of the chi of the mind. What I do is manipulate the chi of the body." While the answer struck me as a total fudge, what caught my interest was that he didn't *deny* a relationship between what he was doing and hypnosis. The seed had been planted!

I didn't stick with that teacher for too long as I rapidly concluded that his 'art' was more about an ego trip for him rather than about helping his students develop something of value. However, I do have to thank him for inadvertently starting me out on a journey that has shaped the course of my life in some truly remarkable ways. Today, I am most widely known in the world as a 'hypnotist' and expert on the mechanics of hypnosis. But, as I say, this has all come about by accident.

My journey from that point has led me to explore hypnosis, human perception and the psychology of influence from within a range of different contexts: teaching, manual therapy, street hypnosis, sales, theatrical performance, hypnotherapy, developmental coaching and more. Early on I took trainings in hypnosis from hypnotherapists, corporate trainers and performers, but I most often found their explanations as to what hypnosis was and how it worked no more plausible than the explanation of chi manipulation I'd received from my first chi gong teacher.

Though I had been studying and exploring with hypnosis in various forms for many years already, the origins of this book lay in my street hypnosis days of 2008–09. This was the period during which it became clear that my approach to hypnosis had become quite distinctive. Whilst other street hypnotists on the scene were pulling people's arms and shouting 'sleep', I was sitting quietly in the corner gently talking people into mind altering experiences without any thoughts of the hypnotic 'induction' often said to be essential. Some other hypnotists asked me how I was achieving these effects. Good question! I had never thought to unpack my approach until asked to do so, and I therefore got busy figuring out how to teach what I was doing.

At this time I was also a practicing hypnotherapist, but this was not the context in which I was being asked to explain and teach hypnosis. I essentially started writing this book in 2009 as 'The Street Hypnosis Handbook'. I left it for a little over a decade as other priorities took over and I became more in demand as a trainer, changework facilitator and coach. It's only now in 2020, over a decade later, that I have been able to (willing to?) carve out the time to finally realise it, and only with the help of my friend Ian Rowland and his keen editorial mind.

Inevitably, the book has changed. It is no longer 'The Street Hypnosis Handbook', but instead a book on how hypnosis actually works and how *you* can become highly adept (or even more highly adept) at facilitating it. That said, its origins leave their finger prints, and that I shall explain.

What This Book Is, and Is Not, About

This book is simply about hypnosis: what it is, how it works and how to get good at doing it. For me, hypnosis at its simplest is about moving someone from their current experience of reality into a different one *via strategic communication*. This shift in 'reality' could be almost anything: a hand stuck to a head, an experience of amnesia, a hallucination, a deep sense of inner strength, relief from chronic pain, an opening to possibility, a state of motivation (to change or to purchase — depending on the context).

The kind of shift in reality you want to evoke will, of course, depend upon context and intention but, regardless of what the shift might be, the principles and skills involved in its facilitation remain largely the same. It is these principles and skills that this book is about.

So this book is very much about hypnosis. What it is *not* at all about is 'hypnosis *for* x'. It is not about hypnosis for change, hypnosis for pain relief, hypnosis for performance, hypnosis for performance enhancement, 'covert' hypnosis for sales or for any other specific context.

I also want to state emphatically that I do not claim Hypnosis Without Trance (HWT) to be a special *type* of hypnosis, as opposed to hypnosis *with* trance. While there certainly is a different stylistic flavour, the real claim here is that *all* hypnosis is, in reality, 'without trance' regardless. Or, to put it another way, hypnosis is not (and has never been) predicated upon any particular special state or states (named 'trance' or otherwise). HWT is about working directly with the cognitive processes that create our experience of the moment, so if you want to shape an experience of 'trance' (for whatever reason), HWT will *help you get better at doing that too.*

Throughout this book, we focus on simple examples of what can be considered classic 'hypnotic phenomena' to illustrate the principles, strategies and tactics of hypnotic facilitation. Many of these examples were chosen during the books genesis as a 'street hypnosis' guide. However, as these phenomena also serve perfectly as vehicles for unpacking mechanisms, principles, strategies and tactics at their most fundamental level, they have remained as the examples of choice. There are also some examples drawn from the world of professional hypnotic changework but, regardless of the context, none of these are offered to be *learned*, only to be *learned from.*

Who This Book Is For

This book is for anyone who has an interest in how hypnosis works, especially those looking to develop real skill with hypnotic facilitation. Throughout the book we look at hypnosis on many different levels, from the top levels of philosophy and principles, down to the ground levels of strategy, tactics and specific manoeuvres.

The focus of the book is very much what might be termed 'formal hypnosis'. This is hypnotic facilitation where explicit frames have been set around what is to happen, i.e.

the people being facilitated know that the game is afoot! I am aware that some who have bought this book will have a specific interest in 'covert' and 'conversational' hypnosis. Whilst not the primary focus of this book, we will necessarily be covering aspects of this because pre-framing for 'overt' hypnosis relies on 'covert' hypnotic communication. Even if you are only interested in covert hypnosis, it's better to *start* by studying overt hypnosis to learn all the basic structures and principles. Once you have developed some expertise in this area, you'll be in a good position to develop your interest in covert hypnosis.

What About Therapy and Changework?

I began using hypnosis professionally in the context of changework/therapy in 2006. I'll be honest here: when I started out — in spite of years of experience using hypnotic communication in manual therapy, teaching martial arts and performing as a magician — I was really *not* very good at the changework.

Many people teach simple 'therapy' protocols, many of which have much that is good about them. However, these protocols don't usually instil the high levels of adaptability and creativity you need to work with a broad range of clients and their individual requirements. My view of changework (I have never framed what I do as 'therapy') is that it should be regarded as a rich craft in and of itself. Whilst it is definitely augmented through its integration with hypnotic communication and facilitation, given its depth and breadth, it would require a dedicated book of its own to really do it justice. For this reason, hypnotherapy and/or changework are not covered in this book beyond occasional illustrative examples.

However, if hypnotherapy and/or changework *are* your game, do not overlook what this book has to offer. You will learn much that will serve you in your work: much about moving minds and shifting attention; much about adaptation and improvisation. Even the examples from street hypnosis may have more value than you imagine simply because *memorable and impactful hypnotic experiences can change lives in and of themselves.*

As I write this, I recall an occasion some years back when I was at a complimentary therapies exhibition, walking about and giving impromptu hypnosis demonstrations. Back then, I often created an experience for people of my hypnotherapy business card sticking between their finger and thumb so they couldn't drop it (I now rarely do this as I don't need to promote my services in this way). After this event, I received a lengthy email from someone I had taken into the experience. She told me about ongoing problems with her state of mind that had grown so great as to have her considering suicide... but that had now changed. The line that sticks in my memory from that email was: "I want to thank you because what you showed me has given me hope."

As part of my street hypnosis protocol, I would always look to making the experience meaningful in a way that served the person I was working with. Working this way I could take what might otherwise be mere 'hypnotic stunts' and turn them into potentially life changing gifts. And I'm sure I don't need to spell out how this might be applicable to those in the world of hypnotherapy and/or changework! Anyhows, suffice it to say that if you are interested in changing lives with hypnosis, you will find a lot of useful information in this book even though changework is not the primary focus.

Overview

Perhaps due to my level of immersion in the topic, I tend to see all that comprises 'hypnosis' as a network of nodes rather than as a series of steps or stages. However, I am aware that such a view isn't always the most useful in terms of helping people to learn it. I have therefore done my best (though it runs contrary to my nature) to organise the material into a linear sequence more conducive to successful learning. And so...

We start out creating a pitch to play on through unpacking some basic definitions and laying out the fundamental principles. Then we dive deep into pragmatics by unpacking the structure of a basic hypnotic facilitation from beginning to end. Following that we get into the nitty gritty of hypnotic communication and suggestion structuring at the level of strategy, tactics and specific manoeuvres. Finally, we round things out with some nuances and assorted bits of business for bringing finesse to your game. There is also a booklet entitled 'Hypnosis Sessions: Full Transcripts With Notes' that refers back to key aspects and elements explored throughout the book. You can download this free of charge from my website: www.hypnosiswithouttrance.com/transcripts

I have aimed to be pretty thorough (though with a tight focus), but I am aware that you may find yourself with an unanswered question or two at the end. Should this be so, you can ask these via the private HWT Facebook group, which you can join via HypnosisWithoutTrance.com. This is a free resource for anyone sincere about learning HWT or hypnosis in general.

A Note on Terminology and Grammar

I want to briefly say something about terminology and grammar. Like any field, hypnosis has accrued its own particular nomenclature over time. In this book there are many places where I have departed from the standard terminology and introduced my own. Where I have done so it's because I felt the old terminology was misleading in some disadvantageous (though often subtle) way.

One notable example is switching out the traditional term 'subject' for the term 'co-operator'. This is to reflect the understanding and attitude that formal hypnosis is more about a co-operative and collaborative partnership than it is about a dominant hypnotist doing something to a passive 'subject'. Running alongside this I often use the term 'operator' instead of 'hypnotist', giving us the pairing of operator and the co-operator (think pilot and co-pilot) working collaboratively in the shaping of the new hypnotic realities we are looking to create. Occasionally, I have also used the term 'hypnotee' where 'co-operator' didn't quite seem to fit. That said, I have used 'subject' a few times when referring to more traditional ways of doing things.

Another example is the use of the term 'hypnotic facilitation' in place of 'hypnotism'. This is simply to reflect the dynamism of the work. Good hypnotic facilitation is a 'real-time game' where we pay attention to what is unfolding in each moment and adjust accordingly towards our outcomes. It is most certainly not some inflexible, stock process that is 'done to' a person. My sense is 'hypnotic facilitation' is a term more usefully connotative of the dynamism that lays at the heart of our approach than is the term 'hypnotism'.

There are no doubt many other instances and what I would suggest is: whenever you notice departures from classic terminology, stop and *feel in* to the difference between the classical terms and the HWT choice. What differences in *connotation* do you pick up? What do the new and old terms *evoke* within you and what is the difference? And there is a bonus to doing this: learning to really pay attention to words and wording on this level *will* make you a better hypnotic communicator by increasing your sensitivity to the subtleties of language.

Regarding grammar, I may play fast and loose with it at times, *especially* in the examples of hypnotic languaging itself. In hypnotic communication, we use language *not* to convey information but instead to direct attention, lead cognition and evoke sense and feeling. This means we often use odd grammatical structuring that might stick out on paper but goes completely under the radar within the context of the facilitation.

Another challenge in writing hypnotic language is that it is as much about the non-verbal and tonal components as it is the verbal. For this reason you will see weird punctuation in almost all the examples of hypnotic languaging given in the book. This is always an attempt (albeit imperfect) to convey a little more of the feel and flow of the hypnotic languaging. My recommendation here is that you avoid any attempts to decipher the punctuation rules and instead simply allow yourself to go with it however it flows.

OK, that's about that... let's dive into 'Hypnosis Without Trance: How Hypnosis Really Works'.

— James Tripp, January 2021

1

DEFINITIONS AND

PRINCIPLES

1. Definitions and Principles

Defining Hypnosis Without Trance

In many ways, learning any skill or craft is much like putting together a jigsaw puzzle — there are many pieces that make up a coherent whole, and an almost infinite number of possibilities in terms of where to begin and how best to proceed. With jigsaws, people often start with edge-pieces. Perhaps the clearest 'edge-piece' I can offer with regard to learning Hypnosis Without Trance (HWT) is a useable, working definition:

> *Hypnosis is the engagement of beliefs and imagination, via verbal and nonverbal communication, to facilitate an altered subjective reality.*

Now, as you might expect (given the title of this book) there is nothing said here about any kind of 'special state' that is unique to hypnosis or required to make it work — because this is *not* really how hypnosis works. The fundamental position of HWT is that hypnosis works through the creative engagement of people's everyday cognitive faculties. Developing the skills and understandings to work strategically with these faculties towards interesting and useful outcomes is what HWT is all about.

If you read this initial definition through a few times (and really take it in) you'll likely notice that there is a fair bit of richness to it that warrants unpacking. So let's look at the main elements, the important ideas it contains, and how they are relevant to us as facilitators of hypnotic experiences.

Engagement of Beliefs

Hypnosis is the engagement of beliefs...

I cannot emphasise too strongly that the primary element that makes hypnosis work is the successful engagement (and modification) of beliefs. This is skilled work and will be the focus of much of this book.

To make sense of this, it is important to understand that most of what we human beings perceive as 'reality' isn't merely 'that which is going on around us', but is instead an *interpretation* and *experiential rendering* of what's going on. To put it more succinctly:

> We do not live in the world as it is, but in the world as it occurs to us – as our minds make it up to be!

Essentially, in every waking moment of our lives, we are neuropsychologically pulling the raw data of our senses through a matrix of unconscious beliefs, and so shaping our experience of that moment.

To illustrate this, when we see an object we'd identify as a chair, we don't just see the object, we 'see' our understanding of it and its role in the life of human beings. A bat would experience it very differently. When my wife sees a rodent, she gets 'the creeps', whereas my daughter will experience 'cute'. What makes for the difference in experience? Not the 'thing out there' but how the mind makes up the experience.

People say 'seeing is believing' but, in reality, believing is seeing (or, even more accurately, 'experiencing'). This understanding is fundamentally important to us as hypnotists and we shall be exploring it more deeply as we move through the book. For now (and to put it very simply): when we believe something as reality, we tend to experience it as reality — and that, in turn, can have 'real world' effects.

To illustrate this, consider the placebo effect. Clinical trials have shown that patients given 'fake' medicine (with no active ingredients) often respond as if the medicine were effective *provided they believe it is*. For another example, anthropologists have studied cultures in which a 'Medicine Man' is believed to have great power. If the Medicine Man simply tells someone they are infected by an evil spirit and will be dead by morning, they may in fact die overnight.

In our work 'bending reality' we won't be giving people fake medicine or telling them they're going to die (you know, it's an ethical issue!), but we most certainly will be engaging their beliefs in helping them to create new, interesting and useful 'realities'. Sometimes this will be for fun, exploration and entertainment and sometimes to help them to achieve positive and significant shifts in their ongoing experience in life. For me, the latter is where the real magic resides.

Imagination

...and imagination...

The second element of our definition refers to the engagement of *imagination*. There's no doubt that human imagination is, or can be, immensely powerful. If someone can imagine something (with your help), they are halfway to perceiving it as a new reality. At the risk of stating the obvious, people can't perceive what they can't even imagine.

Imagination is a powerful nexus of influence for us as hypnotic facilitators because it directly engages the neurophysiology of our hypnotic 'co-operators' (the people that we are engaging with hypnotically). Indeed, if we take it that the 'mind' is emergent from the 'brain', we could say that every act of imagination essentially is an act of neurophysiology! What this means to us as hypnotic facilitators is is that, through directing and/or leading a person's imagination, we are literally affecting how their mind and body is working in that moment.

You can demonstrate this for yourself right now. Imagine that you are holding a lemon (and really do this — read this slowly and immerse yourself as fully as you can in the imaginative experience). You can see it in your hand. You can see its yellow colour and feel its texture. Now imagine cutting into the lemon with a knife so the juice oozes out and may even squirt a little at you. Imagine bringing the lemon up to your mouth and biting deeply into its flesh so you feel the juice filling your mouth and taste that sharp 'tang' of fresh lemon. As you exercise your imagination in this way, you will probably find yourself beginning to salivate somewhat. Whilst this may not work for everyone just through reading it through (fixed, written words are no substitute for a live, dynamic hypnotic facilitation) — full immersion in this as an imagined experience invariably creates changes to salivation and mouth sensation for all normally functioning human beings. (If it worked for you, please try not to drool on to these pages! And if it didn't, were you really imagining it fully or were you more caught up in thoughts and evaluations about it?)

Here's another exercise you can try (and again, take your time to really imagine it). Imagine a fly landing on your nose right now. Imagine this fly walking around a little on your nose, taking a few ticklish steps. Imagine this happening now... and you may begin to feel a need... or the tickling of a desire... to scratch your nose. Isn't that a curious thing? (Don't scratch it yet!)

These two simple exercises show us how imagination can create vivid experiences that become reality (real salivation and real itching). As hypnotists, this is a major facet of our craft — helping people create new realities from the inside-out through the capturing and leading of imagination. Once we connect with the possibilities inherent within this, we can find ourselves connecting with something that can seem close to magic itself.

Verbal and Nonverbal Communication

...via verbal and nonverbal communication...

With hypnosis, we are interested in shifting people's experiences of reality, but we wouldn't call all such shifts in experience 'hypnotic'. People's perceptions of reality can be altered in numerous ways that have nothing whatsoever to do with hypnosis. For example, maybe a person has a fever or has been indulging their penchant for 'recreational pharmaceuticals' — personal reality *will* likely alter but no hypnosis has taken place. So what makes *our* reality shifting 'hypnotic'? The means by which we affect the shifts!

As hypnotists, our craft is the creation of shifts in perceived reality *strategically* using two interrelating sets of tools: verbal and nonverbal communication.

'Verbal', as we use the term here, covers *what* you say — the words themselves.

'Nonverbal' covers the *way* you say those words (tonality, tempo and emphasis) along with all the other ways in which we communicate with one another: gestures, actions, facial expressions, body language and so on.

We will be going into both of these areas extensively later on in this book. For now, it is enough to be aware that the most effective hypnotists are adept at the *strategic* and *tactical* use of both verbal and nonverbal communication in the facilitation of their work. I emphasise this because, although words and word choices are unquestionably important in the practice of hypnosis, they are often overly focused upon in some approaches to hypnosis (e.g. 'script based' approaches aka 'scriptnosis') to the exclusion of the non-verbal. This will *always* be to the overall detriment of the work as it leaves out the *most* powerful means to influence people at the deepest levels.

Facilitation

...to facilitate...

In the world of classic hypnosis, the verb 'to hypnotise' has been a long-standing fixture of the standard nomenclature. I will be clear here in stating that I do *not* think the use of this verb is either useful or particularly accurate.

The reality is that formal hypnosis is not really a thing that is done *to* someone; it is something that is done *with* them. What unfolds during a hypnotic session is a collaboration between hypnotist and hypnotee — operator and co-operator — and each has their role. The role of the hypnotee is simple: to engage as directed. The role of the hypnotist is to *facilitate* that engagement, directing the process in such a way as to create the desired results (a specific and/or useful shift in subjective reality). The important point here is that you as the hypnotist neither *create* the change nor *make* it happen. The hypnotee creates their subjective shift in reality entirely from within their own mind and imagination. They have the power, not you. You simply facilitate the process (and I'll be showing you how to do this).

This may come as a disappointment to those looking to 'mind control' people into doing their bidding (perhaps firing Mesmer-rays from their eyes as they go). If this is you, you may not wish to read on, as this book is very much about facilitation, not domination.

The Alteration of Subjective Experience

...an altered subjective reality.

The final part of our definition refers to an altered subjective reality. This can take many different forms and will obviously vary with context. If you're entertaining people, you might wish to facilitate an interesting and uncommon experience (such as your co-operator's hand stick to a table or their name temporarily gone from their mind). If you're conducting a hypnotherapy session, it will be more about shifting your client's perceptions in order to help them to transcend a problem.

In Hypnosis Without Trance the focus on the end-goal of 'an altered subjective reality' is absolutely fundamental to our approach, and this raises an interesting distinction between the traditional 'trance' paradigm and the HWT approach. In the traditional 'trance' paradigm, what is possible in terms of results is always connected to a loose metric referred to as 'depth of trance', so if something isn't happening, it is considered to be a sign that 'trance' must be 'deepened'. This leads to a preoccupation with ensuring that the hypnotee is indeed in a 'trance state', where the development of 'trance' is monitored via the tracking of *trance analogues*: subtle changes in skin colour, breathing pattern, muscle tone and so forth.

Now, there is a valid principle here of *paying attention to feedback* (a key element of all good hypnotic facilitation, and strongly emphasised in HWT) but, unless the outcome is the trance state in and of itself, it is essentially looking in the wrong place and making the overall process highly inefficient.

Here's an example. Imagine that we wish to facilitate in someone an experience of their arm lifting up all by itself. Under the 'trance model' this would be considered a 'trance phenomenon' — a product of 'hypnotic trance' and therefore the initial aim would be to 'induce' a sufficient 'depth of trance' for the suggested phenomenon (arm lifting) to happen. If we operate by this paradigm, our main goal is trance so that is what we go for (using 'trance analogues' as feedback if we are doing it skilfully).

In Hypnosis Without Trance, however, we regard the shifts in reality that we create as a product of the engagement of neuropsychological faculties and *not* as a product of any special or unusual state. This frees us to go directly for the phenomenon of arm lifting without having to go via trance, and our feedback becomes less about 'trance analogues' (which have nothing to do with lifting arms) and more about seeing muscles responding and our co-operator's subjective reports.

This 'arm lifting' example highlights a problem with the classical 'state based' approaches: the incongruence between ideas of 'trance' and the desired outcome. For an arm to lift, muscles must engage, but traditional 'trance' is often associated with *profound relaxation*. By using such an 'induction' we would be *reducing* muscle tone initially only to then have to increase it again. It's more efficient to go directly for the arm lift, thus going in the appropriate direction right from the start.

Also, in hypnotherapy, traditional trance might be the last direction you would wish to go with a 'depressed' client — you may instead wish to bring them to a more enlivened state. On the other hand, traditional 'trance' *could* be great for someone with anxiety. Ultimately, it's all about considering what is going to be useful for the client rather than adopting a 'one state fits all' approach.

With HWT we are looking to shape the desired end states *directly*, rather than focusing our efforts on 'inducing' a 'one size fits all' trance that may *not* actually be a good fit at all. In bypassing this chasing of 'trance', we are able to not only be a lot more efficient but also considerably more adaptive to the feedback that actually counts (signs indicating the development of the true outcome), thereby empowering us to more effectively steer the process.

Simply put, we monitor how the desired alteration of experience is occurring (and we'll be looking at how we do this later) and, if it is shaping up nicely we are 'game on'. If not, we consider how to precision trouble-shoot (not just 'deepen trance') and course correct to get the engagement and results we are looking for. Essentially, we focus on what counts for our outcome and avoid being pulled off the scent by the 'red herring' of classic trance.

So, that's our Hypnosis Without Trance working definition for hypnosis. Before we continue our learning journey, I invite you to take another few moments to savour it now we've surveyed its component parts:

Hypnosis is the engagement of beliefs and imagination, via verbal and nonverbal communication, to facilitate an altered subjective reality.

Formal/Overt v Covert Hypnosis

Having outlined a foundational definition for 'hypnosis' from within the Hypnosis Without Trance paradigm, there is a further distinction worth spotlighting at this point: *formal/overt versus covert hypnosis*. This is worth taking a few moments with because whilst there are many overlapping principles between the two, in their pure forms, the flavour and feel of the two are quite different.

Formal/Overt Hypnosis

Formal/Overt hypnosis is defined as any act of hypnosis that takes place with the hypnotee's full awareness and consent. The intention to facilitate hypnosis is openly stated, and the co-operator is invited to engage with it (they may, of course, freely decline). It is in this sense that it is 'overt' — nothing is hidden. It is worth noting here that the term 'formal' denotes only that it is being openly recognised and labelled as hypnosis (or similar 'big because' — a concept we'll look at later), and has nothing to do with being in a formal *setting*, such as an office or clinic.

Covert Hypnosis

Covert hypnosis is defined as hypnosis that takes place without the hypnotee's awareness and consent. So, if someone is utilising the principles and communication tools of hypnosis to influence a person's state of mind, behaviour or choices without their informed consent, then this would be covert hypnosis. Obviously, this leads to some interesting ethical concerns, which we will *not* be addressing here.

Even though covert and conversational hypnosis were my 'first loves', in this book we are *exclusively concerned with overt/formal hypnosis*. However, if your interest is in the covert and conversational, there is still much that you will learn from what we will explore as the underlying principles are essentially the same. Indeed, it is way easier to be effective with covert hypnosis if you first become adept at overt hypnosis. It is also worth being aware that effective overt hypnosis involves a lot of covert hypnotic elements as part of its process — particularly at the early stages of frame setting and engineering buy-in as well as any work that empowers and enables the cooperator after the formal process has *apparently* closed.

A point worth noting here is that both overt/formal hypnosis and covert hypnosis require the *active engagement* of the hypnotee. With overt/formal hypnosis, this can be explicitly requested and even coached. With covert hypnosis, attention and proactive engagement must be *captured* by subtler means. This is *not* 'mind control', just effective use of communication to foster engagement and absorption — effective *influence* yes, mind *control* no.

Maps and Belief Systems

"Who is the great magician who makes the grass green?"
— Traditional Zen koan.

A person's belief system is all that they believe to be true about life, the universe and everything. It is the sum total of the sense they have made about what is or isn't so, is or isn't right, what's possible and what's not (etcetera), encompassing every aspect of life that they know or know of. People operate out of their belief system 24/7 — there is nowhere else they can ever come in any and all of their engagements with the world. Understood like this, a person's belief system is, in essence, their 'map of the world' — the map by which they navigate life. Good maps lead to effective navigation, less good maps less so.

It's important to understand this concept if you intend to be an effective hypnotist because you *always* need to work *with* your client's 'map of the world'. If what you present to them is a bad fit for their 'map', it *will* be rejected and the work will go nowhere useful. On the flip-side, *you* also need effective 'maps' of hypnosis and the human change and development to assist you in the navigation of your craft and to inform your choices in each moment of hypnotic facilitation. So, there are two sets of maps that are relevant for us: operator-side maps and cooperator-side maps, and how we manage their intersection is important.

Let's look a little more deeply into this. Back in our unpacking of the HWT definition, I noted: *We do not live in the world as it is, but in the world as it occurs to us — as our minds make it up to be!*

Beyond the tight confines of hypnosis, I have sometimes called this 'the first transformative truth', because a deep understanding of it can free us from all manner of reality tunnels and cherished truths that have kept us bound in limited patterns of response in our lives. But what does it really mean? These words from neurophysiologist Sir John Echols, who won a Nobel prize, provide much illumination:

> "I want you to know that there are no colours in the real world. There are no fragrances in the real world and there's no beauty and there's no ugliness. Out there, beyond the limits of our perceptual apparatus, is the erratically ambiguous and ceaselessly flowing quantum soup. And we're almost like magicians in that in the very act of perception we take that quantum soup and we convert it into the experience of material reality in our ordinary everyday waking state of consciousness."

To me these are truly beautiful and illuminating words, and are of incredible importance to anyone wishing to understand the deepest nature of this craft we call hypnosis. Why? Because, as we have discussed, our work is to influence people's subjective experience of reality. Echols is elegantly describing how we all *create* our reality in the first place. As he says, it's an almost *magical* process.

Think about what is being said here: every day, in your ordinary waking state of consciousness, you *create* your reality. You turn what's going on around you into the phenomenological experience of 'this moment'. Or, to answer the koan:

> You are the great magician who makes the grass green!

But how are you doing this? A full neurological explanation is not only beyond the scope of this book but also still far from being fully nailed down by those who do such nailing down. Aside from that, this type of explanation wouldn't serve us especially well. Instead, we're better off referring to the work of 17th century philosopher René Descartes.

In his essay, "Meditations on First Philosophy", Descartes considered a rather interesting question: what could he know with *absolute certainty* about life, the universe and the world around him? The answer (spoiler alert!) turned out to be... not much. Descartes realised that, since perceptions can be flawed and almost everything *could* just be a delusion, every aspect of what he regarded as 'reality' was open to doubt. The only thing he *couldn't* doubt, he decided, was that he himself existed — because he had to exist in order to be considering the question. He expressed this as, "Cogito, ergo sum": I think, therefore I am. The work of Descartes and other philosophers has shown us that no-one has access to a true, objective, external reality. Nobody experiences the world 'as it is'. Instead, what you regard as 'reality' is a bunch of raw sense-data pulled through a set of beliefs in your mind that shape it into what you experience in each moment.

We are not born with these beliefs — they are the product of learning, experience, passive exposure to the ideas of others (family, wider culture and so on), conclusions you've arrived at regarding how you think life works, how you see yourself and how you see other people: a melting pot in your head that creates the perception that it's actually 'out there' in the world. Through our learning and experience we each create an individual map that is unique to us and us alone. You have your map in your mind, I have my map in mine and everyone else you meet has a map in theirs.

To reiterate, we need these maps to navigate life — without them we'd be lost. This is, after all, what maps are for. When you're navigating, you use a map to figure out where you are, where you want to get to and how to get there. Your mental map works in much the same way. It's how you make sense of your reality and navigate your way through it. However, it's important to remember that 'the map is not the territory' (a pithy little saying from the work of Alfred Korzybski) and that your beliefs are *not* reality *even* when they are shaping your experience of it!

It's clear that the belief systems that reside in human minds vary a great deal. This is why we have so many different beliefs about, for example, politics, religion and which is the best flavour of ice-cream (even though it's *obviously*

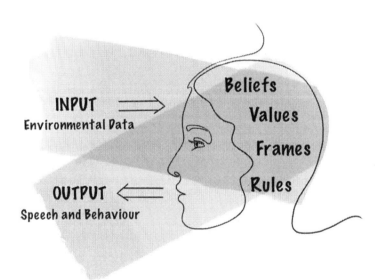

salted caramel and anyone who thinks otherwise is clearly mad). More importantly for anyone interested in hypnosis, these beliefs can be *shaped* and *changed*. When you successfully create a hypnotic shift with someone, you have facilitated a shift in their neurophysiology; a major part of which occurs within the neurologically encoded beliefs that are shaping the person's experience of reality.

One simple example of how beliefs come into play with hypnosis is the *idea* of hypnosis itself. When we introduce the idea of potentially doing some hypnosis with a person, we will be activating and necessarily engaging with all of their beliefs about 'hypnosis'. For some this will create a barrier (perhaps they are actively sceptical or afraid that to 'succumb' would mean they are weak minded etc.). For others it will create a bridge (because they believe it is a real phenomenon that they are eager to experience). For this reason, it is usually a good idea to note their reactions when you bring the idea up and even explicitly ask them about their beliefs regarding the topic. Your aim here is to help them make sense of what is going to happen in a way that fits their 'map of the world', *not* try to convince them of something that just isn't a good fit.

Let's look at an example of someone who has positive beliefs about hypnosis and is keen to engage. In this instance, we could perform a ritual (this is really what a classic hypnosis induction is, in the HWT view) that *means* they are 'hypnotised'. We can frame some aspect of their experience (change in breathing pattern, sense of calm etc.) as being signs of hypnosis, and so we engender the belief that *hypnosis is happening*. Because they already believe hypnosis has the power to create highly unusual effects, and now believe that they are 'in hypnosis', we can leverage that belief to suggest that an unusual effect may now happen (such as their hand being now stuck immovably to the table), and combine that with an imaginative description to shape the experience of the effect itself.

Put simply, your co-operator believes in hypnosis, believes they are are hypnotised and that hypnosis has the power to stick their hand to the table. As a result, when you suggest that this will happen *and* imaginatively shape the experience of it happening, that is exactly what their physiology creates as a result: their hand sticks to the table. The *belief* creates the experience of a *reality* in which their hand is stuck to the table in a rather intriguing way.

To be absolutely clear, this has *nothing* to do with being weak-minded or credulous, it is simply a function of beliefs and how they work. We are *all*, *always* operating and creating the present moment through our beliefs — both the person who 'cannot be hypnotised' and the person who can manifest hypnotic experiences readily are just as tightly bound by whatever beliefs are at play in the moment. Both are equally weak in succumbing to beliefs or, alternatively, equally strong in creating a solid reality from them.

In his cult classic 'Prometheus Rising', Robert Anton Wilson offers us a neat device for thinking about the relationship between beliefs and experience of reality. Following in the footsteps of American yogi Leonard Orr, Wilson describes two distinct faculties of mind he calls the 'thinker' and the 'prover'. Wilson suggests that 'whatever the thinker thinks, the prover proves'. Essentially, whatever you believe, your 'neuro-psycho-physiology' will get busy selecting and/or creating evidence to validate it. In other words, you may come to regard something as real and true because you first of all *believed* it.

So, let's put this into the context of our previously given definition of hypnosis:

Hypnosis is the engagement of beliefs and imagination, via verbal and nonverbal communication, to facilitate an altered subjective reality.

Note again that last part: 'to facilitate an altered subjective reality'. The fact that people don't have perceptual access to *any* type of objective reality — only a *subjective* reality shaped by a *belief system* — is what makes this alteration possible. As a hypnotist, your role is to access your co-operator's belief system so you can utilise it, modify it or extend it in ways that both allow for and create the desired experiential shift. The process is supported and augmented through the strategic directing of attention and leading of cognition and imagination. In short, we are directing minds to shape immediate (and sometimes ongoing) experience. This is what Hypnosis Without Trance is all about!

About Hypnotic Trance

Having discussed belief systems and mental maps, I want to discuss the notion that shapes much of the classical thinking regarding hypnosis: 'hypnotic trance'.

In what might be called the 'classic' paradigm of hypnosis, the hypnotist's primary role is the placing of the 'subject' into a *special state* by means of a process called 'induction'. This special state, which is sometimes simply referred to as 'hypnosis' and sometimes as 'hypnotic trance', is thought to render the 'subject' open to suggestion in a way they wouldn't be otherwise. It is considered the *reason* for the hypnotic phenomena.

The notion of a 'special state' goes back to the time of Franz Anton Mesmer and his practice of healing by 'animal magnetism' (more popularly known as Mesmerism). Mesmer's aim was *not* to create a state of suggestibility but to influence healing, for which he gained a considerable reputation. Indeed, his fame grew to such an extent throughout Paris that in 1784 King Louis XVI commissioned the Royal Academy of Sciences to investigate Mesmer's work. The conclusion of the investigating committee was that Mesmer's healing effects were *not* in fact the result of magnetism (animal or otherwise), but were instead attributable entirely to suggestion and imagination.

Though this led to the destruction of Mesmer's professional reputation, some were still curious enough about the effectiveness of his work to embark upon their own investigations. Notably amongst these was Scottish physician James Braid, who concluded that the 'Mesmeric state' (so often observed in Mesmer's patients as he worked) must be creating the suggestibility that was seen to be in play. I'm going to suggest here that in reaching this conclusion Braid somewhat put the cart before the horse; that it was those sufficiently responsive to suggestion who were taking the suggestions to go into the Mesmeric state!

Now, despite much research and evidence debunking this 'trance' model (see Hypnosis: 'The Cognitive-Behavioural Perspective' by Spanos and Chaves if you have an appetite for such research), the idea of 'trance' is still dominant in the world of 'lay hypnosis' and hypnotherapy. Indeed, this can be a sensitive topic for some adherents to state-based models. Fortunately we need not get caught up in the debate as our primary interest is with what is *useful* rather than what is scientifically *correct*. So, *is* the trance model useful? Having explored this extensively, my own conclusion is that trance theory is useful *up to a point* but that ultimately it hinders more than it helps. To borrow from author Brad Blanton:

> "Yesterday's liberating insight is today's jail of stale explanation."

> (Brad Blanton, 'Radical Honesty: How to Transform Your Life by 'Telling the Truth' — this is not a book recommendation, by the way!)

For me, the whole notion of a hypnotic trance fairly rapidly became such a 'jail'; incarcerating me in an unnecessarily limited set of possibilities that hindered both my efficacy and development as a hypnotist (and I have seen it similarly restrict many others as well). Let me explain why.

My first reservation about the trance theory is the notion that in order to hypnotise someone you have to somehow get them into the correct state. What's more, this state must be induced to the requisite *depth*. Appealing as this notion may be to some, my experience (along with much contemporary academic research) suggests this cherished notion of depth is not only fictitious but also irrelevant in terms of the successful evocation of hypnotic phenomena. In the HWT approach we avoid the red herrings of 'trance' and 'depth' and instead focus on quality of engagement — is the co-operator appropriately engaged with the process or not? If they are, results will ensue. If they are not, they won't. There is no 'depth' involved. The advantage to this approach is that, should the engagement be off, we can troubleshoot *how specifically* it is off, and coach our co-operator in their engagement accordingly. This is quite different from trying to generically 'deepen' more in the hope that it fixes what's off.

My second reservation concerns the notion that specific hypnotic phenomena are associated with specific depths of trance as this is demonstrably not the case. If you do a lot of hypnosis with enough curiosity about what is actually happening, you *will* find plenty of evidence to contradict this idea. You'll find there are times when you get what are classically said to be 'deep trance phenomena' quite easily, with no 'trance induction' or 'deepening' whatsoever. Other times you have all the signs of 'deep trance' and yet the 'deep trance phenomena' are just not happening.

To illustrate the former, I once had someone spontaneously hallucinate a dog as a result of my telling them about *another* time I had someone else do the same (I wasn't intending the result, just telling a story). On another occasion, I simply instructed someone I was working with therapeutically to close their eyes and imagine they were standing over by the door watching themselves sitting in their chair. After the guy opened his eyes he exclaimed aghast, "How did you do that? I was actually stood there by the door looking at myself! How did you do that?" The common denominator here is that both these people perceived me as a credible hypnotist, and had strong buy-in for the notion of hypnosis.

So, the notion of 'depth' just doesn't correspond to what happens in practice — *belief* and *engagement* are what drive the game.

The major problem with this fixation on 'depth' is simply that it leads us to looking in the wrong direction when steering the hypnotic process. For example, if you don't achieve a particular phenomenon by 'post-hypnotic suggestion' (a suggestion given 'in trance' to be enacted 'upon awakening'), you might be inclined to 'put the subject back into hypnosis' and attempt to take them 'deeper'. To my mind, this is going down a blind alley. Instead of merely 'deepening', we are much better served by figuring out what needs to happen to better engage our co-operator's *beliefs* and better lead their *imagination*; how to work more successfully with their *maps* and frames in order to get the 'buy in' that we need for the desired effects to occur. Through abandoning the 'trance model' and adopting the strategic process model of Hypnosis Without Trance we are freed to focus in with precision on the specific adjustments required to create the effects that we want.

To sum up: hypnosis isn't about putting someone into a special state. It's about strategically engaging and directing the fundamental cognitive processes that shape everyday perception. To be most effective, you will be best served by keeping your focus on *process* rather than a *state*. This is an important distinction because once you accept that it's a *process*, you open up a lot more choice in in terms of facilitation and can therefore be more adaptive to each client's individual requirements. This, in turn, increases efficacy. The trance model, in contrast, most often creates a closed box that restricts you to a limited number of low impact choices. For this reason, we are choosing to let it go as a basis for our craft.

All that said, there's one last point I want to make about 'trance'. I do sometimes use 'trance' as a convenient label for the type of classic, eyes closed, awareness-turned-inwards, 'going deeper and deeper' presentation of hypnosis. This presentation can sometimes be useful in the context of hypnotherapy, partly because it looks like what people might expect (and can therefore engage their *beliefs* if they have already bought in to the notion) and partly because it can help people release the 'neuromuscular lock' around a stuck pattern of thought or behaviour. This enables people to open to new thinking that was previously shut out, and it is new thinking that is generative of change. Note that this has nothing whatsoever to do with creating 'suggestibility' or anything like that. It's simply about shifting people out of a habitual pattern of response, thereby opening them to the possibilities provided by new thinking and perspective. Neo-Ericksonian hypnosis practitioner Stephen Gilligan calls this 'generative trance', which seems an apt name for it. When we facilitate such work from a process perspective, we have many more options available to us so, somewhat ironically, Hypnosis Without Trance increases skill with trancework.

In this specific context, I believe trance work can be a wonderful thing. However, rather than saying 'you need trance to achieve hypnosis', I believe it's more accurate to say 'we use hypnosis to facilitate trance'. In other words, trance is just one more hypnotic phenomena, like catalepsy, amnesia, analgesia, hallucination and so on.

The Hypnotic Partnership

Because of the way that hypnosis is often portrayed in films and on TV, many people think hypnosis is something you 'do' to someone else. They believe the hypnotist puts people under some sort of influence and can effectively 'control' them like a puppet. But as we dive into the mechanisms of hypnosis we soon find that this view is not only inaccurate but also seriously misleading.

When you facilitate a hypnotic experience with someone, you are not 'doing' anything to them in the *causal* sense. It is not the case that you, the hypnotist, have the active role and your 'subject' is a mere passive puppet. Hypnosis is a process during which you use your communication skills to engage your co-operator's beliefs and imagination. It follows that you and your co-operator *both* have an *active* role to play. I call this relationship between hypnotist and hypnotee the *hypnotic partnership*. The two sides of this partnership have specific, *active* roles.

Your role, as the hypnotist (the *operator*), is to use your verbal and nonverbal communication skills to engage the subject's beliefs and imagination.

The role of the hypnotee (the *co-operator*) is, on a conscious level, to proactively engage with your directions and suggestions and, on a deeper level, to generate the desired shift in their reality (though this will ideally occur to them as a 'happening' rather than a 'doing' on their part).

Once you have successfully engaged your co-operator's beliefs and imagination, *they* create this shift from within. You are not doing something *to* a 'subject'. You are working *with* your co-operator to help them achieve this shift in their perceived reality. They have the power to do this and you are facilitating the process according to your knowledge and expertise.

In order for your co-operator to engage with this process, they need to actively choose to go along with what you suggest (unless you're attempting covert hypnosis, in which case, things get a little more nuanced). For this reason, in conducting formal hypnosis, it helps to let the co-operator know that they have an active and participatory role, not a passive one. Know the kind of engagement you want from your co-operator and be willing to ask for it. Their role involves following your instructions and moving their mind and imagination in the specific ways that you request. The partnership can be likened to a dance. If you try to dance with someone who doesn't want to dance with you, it's simply not going to work even if you happen to be an excellent dancer.

For the hypnotic partnership to be successful, you will need to create a frame of *cooperation* around what you're doing (we'll cover creating such a frame later in the book). If you think of yourself as the all-powerful hypnotist with the ability to control people, there's a good chance you'll not only meet with a lot of push back from the people you work with but also overlook many collaborative options that can enhance your work. With regard to this first point, perhaps understandably, most people don't want to be controlled or manipulated by others, and belief that this is what hypnosis is about is exactly why some people are wary of having anything at all to do with it.

One simple advantage of looking at hypnosis as a co-operative partnership is that it gives you the opportunity to *coach engagement* on the part of the hypnotee. At any point you wish you can find out specifically what they are doing within their mind and request they do more of what is helpful and less of what isn't. This is a far more effective approach to creating results than simply 'deepening trance' and hoping for the best.

Be sure you have taken on board this idea of the hypnotic partnership before you read any further. Hold it in your heart: hypnosis is about *a cooperative relationship*, not power and control. You are learning to be a facilitator of experience, helping your co-operator to commit 100% to the process and, from their inner mind, find the power to generate a shift in their perceived reality.

The Ideodynamic Model

If you remember, our working definition of hypnosis refers to *altered subjective realities*. This is what we are looking to help our hypnotic co-operators to achieve. Some people refer to these altered subjective realities in terms of trance phenomena or even *deep* trance phenomena. We're not going to be using such terms here because, as has already been made clear, we are not operating by the traditional trance model. Instead, I encourage you to think about altered subjective realities in terms of *ideodynamics*.

To the best of my knowledge the term 'ideodynamics' was first introduced to the world of hypnosis by Ernest Rossi and David Cheek in their book 'Mind-body Therapy: Methods of Ideodynamic Healing in Hypnosis'. Rossi and Cheek's work focuses specifically on the application of the *ideomotor* effect in clinical hypnotherapy.

The term 'ideomotor' breaks down to *ideo* meaning 'idea' or 'thought' and *motor* referring to the motor units of muscle. It was first used by William Benjamin Carpenter in his 1852 paper discussing the means by which the Ouija board produced its results. In this paper, Carpenter suggested that muscular movement can be driven by unconscious thoughts and ideas independent of conscious desires or emotions.

We can see this *ideomotor effect* at work in the generation of many classic hypnotic phenomena. Arm levitation is a good example — in response to the idea of lifting, the appropriate muscles engage to make it happen outside of consciousness. Another example might be a hand stuck to a table-top — the effect created by unconscious muscular action in response to suggestion and imagination. It is also

clear that ideomotor action doesn't account for the full
range of 'hypnotic phenomena' (analgesia, hallucination,
emotive effects etc). For this reason, I use the term
'ideodynamics' in a broader sense that covers the full range
of hypnotic effects. This is the HWT ideodynamics model,
as distinct from that of Rossi and Cheek.

In our rendering of ideodynamics, *'ideo'* refers to ideas,
cognitive processes and the engagement of beliefs and
imagination that lies at the core of hypnosis. The *'dynamics'*
part refers to the response that takes place outside of
consciousness as a result of engaging beliefs and
imaginations. To map this out we can divide ideodynamic
phenomena into four basic categories:

- Ideomotor.
- Ideosensory.
- Ideoemotive.
- Ideocognitive.

Let's briefly look at each of these in turn.

Ideomotor

Here, 'motor' refers to 'motor control': muscles moving the body in response to neurological impulses. Many classic hypnotic phenomena involve the ideomotor response. One example would be catalepsy, where the co-operator is able to maintain a limb, or their entire body, in a fixed but effortless position. Other examples would include an 'arm levitation', where the co-operator's hand rises up apparently of its own volition or a 'stick', where some part of the body is apparently stuck to something. These things happen because the hypnotee's beliefs, cognitions and imagination have been engaged in such a way as to initiate a muscular response appropriate to the generation of the effect. The effect that we are aiming for is an experience of something happening all by itself, rather than an experience of volitional action on the part of the co-operator. We seek a *happening* rather than a *doing*.

In hypnotherapy, you can use ideomotor responses as apparent signalling systems to receive messages from the 'unconscious mind'. The practice of *ideomotor signalling* is based on the idea that there is much of relevance within the client's mind that may not be readily accessible in consciousness. In this instance, we can request that the 'unconscious mind' (or the 'part responsible for behaviour x') communicate with us via an ideomotor signal. This could be a finger twitch (such as index finger for 'yes', middle finger for 'no') or a body sway (forward for 'yes', backward for 'no'), or something less binary like a hand lifting only as quickly as some useful insight comes. This kind of work raises an interesting question as to whether it is 'real' (genuine communication with a personified 'unconscious mind' or 'part') or just a useful ritual that works more like a placebo. I feel it lies somewhere between the two.

Ideosensory

An *ideosensory response* works similarly to an *ideomotor response* except that the change effected is in *sensation* rather than muscular action. For example, the hypnotee might experience a tingling sensation or feel that the temperature in the room has gone up or down. They might also lose all feeling (anaesthesia) or just their pain response (analgesia).

It doesn't take a great leap of imagination to see how you could apply this to medical situations. In fact, before the invention of modern anaesthetics, hypnosis was on the rise as a means to provide surgical anaesthesia. Even today, modules on hypnosis are still taught in some dental schools as a possible alternative to anaesthetic, although it doesn't seem to be widely used.

Ideoemotive

Ideoemotive phenomena typically involve the hypnotee experiencing specific changes in emotions, such as joy, euphoria compassion etc. So you might have your co-operator imagine and therefore experience "feeling good for no reason at all... almost as if you're walking on air and everything just seems... right... feeling a deep sense of capability... and that so much is possible for you". Through hypnotic facilitation, you can help your co-operators to generate such emotions. You can also diminish negative emotions, such as anxiety, insecurity and fear. These effects can be used in the creation of new reference experience that can free people from phobias or 'run the charge off' past 'traumatic' events (though it is advisable to combine this with semantic work too — creating new meanings and resultant beliefs). Although not the totality of the work, ideoemotive phenomena have a valuable role hypnotic changework, where they can serve as catalysts for clients achieving quite deep and profound personal shifts.

Ideocognitive

Given that 'ideo' means 'pertaining to cognitive processes', the term 'ideocognitive' is rather circular, but it is a useful category nonetheless. *Ideocognitive* phenomena involve facilitated cognitive processes that generate further cognitive responses. Examples might be amnesia, confusion or (in the context of stage hypnosis) a volunteer feeling compelled to tell the truth or to lie outrageously.

In a changework context I have worked with many individuals suffering from ideocognitive issues. For example, I once worked with someone who had achieved fluency in English as a second language. After getting caught up in some cognitions of self-doubt, they temporarily lost this fluency. Once they worked through those cognitions and neutralised them, their fluency returned.

Ideodynamic Bridging

If you only have one way to approach things you will seriously limit your success. The advantage of the ideodynamics model is that it opens up options within your hypnotic facilitation that would otherwise be hidden from you by more traditional ideas on hypnosis. To be a good hypnotist, it's important to be able to work with each client in terms of their individual cognitive strengths, weaknesses and proclivities, which is where the ideodynamics model, together with the concept of *ideodynamic bridging*, comes in very handy.

When exploring hypnotically with real people, you'll likely find a lot of individual differences regarding which categories of phenomena they can most easily manifest. For example, you might be working with someone who can generate ideomotor and ideosensory responses beautifully but struggles with ideoemotive or ideocognitive ones. Another person might be absolutely perfect for ideomotor demonstrations but not so good with ideosensory ones.

Being aware of these differences helps you to work more adaptively with every hypnotee as an individual, increasing your options in terms of what and how you can hypnotically create with them. For example, suppose you are facilitating a co-operator who doesn't generate ideomotor responses very well. You have been going for the effect of their arm lifting all by itself and it's just not happening. Instead of persisting along a direct ideomotor track, you switch to an ideosensory track and start to shape up a *feeling* of lightness ("...and with each passing moment it *feels* lighter and lighter..."). Should this feeling of lightness take strongly, we will increase the likelihood of a motor effect occurring as a result. This is what we call *ideodynamic bridging*: using a category in which our co-operator is strong to bridge to a phenomenon that might sit in another category that is perhaps more challenging for them.

Here's another example. Suppose you're working with someone who seems to be better at creating ideoemotive responses than ideomotor ones. To create a bridge you might engage their emotions, evoking perhaps a sense of joy or fulfilment, and tie that in to an experience of hands locking together: "and the more you feel this joy and know this joy… the more those fingers lock together… as this joy becomes you."

You can use each type of ideodynamic response as a bridge to one or more of the other types, depending on what kind of responses your co-operator seems to find it easiest to create. This is really useful to know whenever you are giving a demonstration that doesn't seem to be coming together. Instead of 'deepening' more and then trying the same unsuccessful approach over and over again, you simply switch tack and use a different ideodynamic response as a bridge to the effect or phenomena you're aiming to evoke.

I will share a quick anecdote to illustrate this point. During my street hypnosis days, a good friend of mine (the very talented magician Lee Smith) would often tell people I was an excellent hypnotist and could do many incredible things. On one particular occasion I met him in a bar with a couple that he knew (let's call them Paul and Sally). He introduced me to them, saying: "This is James, the hypnotist I was telling you about. James, Paul would love to experience some hypnosis." I sat down with Paul, invited him to place his hand flat on the table and proceeded to facilitate a vivid experience of his hand stuck solidly to the table top in spite of his best conscious efforts to lift it.

After we had finished (and Paul was appropriately amazed), Sally asked "Can you do that to me?" Normally, my rule of thumb is to never let my co-operator know ahead of time what we are going for (as it shuts down my options for manoeuvrability), but on this occasion I acquiesced. I had Sally place her hand down, got her focusing and engaging and started to shape the 'sticking' that she wanted to experience. At this point I thought everything was going pretty well (monitoring both her verbal and nonverbal responses) and felt sufficiently confident to go for a hard challenge. "Go ahead, *try* and un*stick* that hand and find it just *sticks more solidly* to the table". And... she slowly lifted her hand!

Now, that might seem like an instance of 'failure'. However, I could tell from Sally's non-verbal communication that *something* interesting was happening. She didn't just lift her hand in a normal 'conscious' way. She lifted it slowly, with her fingers still spread and her eyes wide and transfixed on the hand. My response was to immediately 'pace' her reality (we'll learn more about how to do this in a later chapter) with the words "That's right... and your hand lifts..." before seeking information on what was happening in her experience; "And as it *slowly* continues to lift... what is it that is happening for you right now?". Her reply was, "It's melting. Melting out like hot Plasticine across the table".

I had gone for an ideomotor phenomenon but got an ideosensory response — a spontaneous visual hallucination. Sally was quite astonished by this as a thing in itself, but I decided to bridge to the original intended outcome nonetheless: "And it melts out like hot Plasticine across the table... and *heavy* hot Plasticine... pulling the hand back down onto the table... into the table... melting into the table and *solidifying into the table*... and when that hand has melted in... as a part of the table... what happens when you try to un*stick* that hand and it is part of the table like this?" I got the hand stick by unusual and idiosyncratic means, using the principle of ideodynamic bridging.

VAKOG

While we're on the subject of people responding differently due to their differing cognitive styles, I will briefly mention a concept from Neurolinguistic Programming/NLP (but rumoured to be from an older source). It is the idea that people mentally process across 5 channels (called 'representational systems' in NLP):

- Visual
- Auditory
- Kinaesthetic
- Olfactory
- Gustatory

I am not going to say too much about this here because it is amply documented elsewhere (just google 'VAKOG' and don't believe everything you read).

You can massively increase your flexibility as a hypnotist by learning to tailor your suggestions to match the various channels (VAK being most important). There can be a world of difference between "*feel* that arm lifting" and "*see* that arm lifting". I'm mentioning VAKOG because it provides a simple template for practising suggestion generation (we will get into hypnotic languaging more fully later).

Ideodynamics and cognitive styles will be important in the next section about *hypnotic loops*: a *physiological response* that produces the *motor, sensory, emotive* or *cognitive* effects I've mentioned. Please bear this in mind. Changes in these areas are changes in *physiology* (though perhaps I should say 'neurophysiology' to eliminate confusion when considering the emotive and cognitive areas). In hypnosis, what's created in the mind is always realised in the body.

The Hypnotic Loop

Before we go any further, please take a moment to remind yourself of our basic (trance-free) definition for hypnosis:

Hypnosis is the engagement of beliefs and imagination, via verbal and nonverbal communication, to facilitate an altered subjective reality.

We've talked about *beliefs* and *imagination*, we've talked about *ideodynamics* but, practically speaking, how does all this hang together to create hypnosis?

When I was considering this question back in my street hypnosis days, I was aware that when hypnotic effects really 'took' they often seemed to somehow feed and perpetuate themselves. It seemed that there were feedback mechanisms in play along with various interacting elements. To this day, I clearly recall the occasion when, with all this in my head, I sat down with a pencil and paper to organise my thoughts. After a few minutes I found myself staring at the schematic that came to be known as the *hypnotic loop*.

The hypnotic loop is a simple, functional representation of how hypnosis works from a *process* perspective. Looking at our diagram we see a self-perpetuating feedback loop of *belief*, *imagination*, *physiology* and *experience*, which we can usefully consider to be the generator of not *just* hypnotic phenomena but all ongoing human experience (phenomenologically speaking). As well as helping us to understand hypnosis in the abstract, the hypnotic loop provides a practical means for mapping the ideodynamic processes that are in play, so as we can be better informed in our real-time choices during hypnotic facilitation work.

Looking at the diagram we can see the four key points are:

Belief > Imagination > Physiology > Experience.

As we see, *beliefs* drive *imagination.*

Next, we see that imagination, in turn, modifies *physiology* (neurophysiology), and this generates the *ideodynamic responses* we've discussed.

The result of the process so far is the generation of an *experience* (this would technically still be raw sense-data at this stage, as it is yet to be shaped into experience by *belief*), which, in turn, confirms and reinforces the initial generative beliefs, thereby completing a single revolution of the loop.

It is important to remember that this model is only a useful simplification. The reality is significantly more complex, but our aim here is not to render absolute truth, only to create a useable map. With this map as our guide, we can see our role as hypnotists as essentially being that of strategically facilitating the formation of these loops within the mind-body systems of our co-operators. Let's look at a practical example to see how this works.

Imagine that you want someone to experience an altered subjective reality — you want to stick their hand to a table-top (my signature coffee shop hypnosis opener)! To do so you need to first engage our co-operator's cognitive processes in such a way that they come to *believe* extraordinary things might be possible. We do this by introducing the notion of hypnosis and getting *buy-in* for doing a little exploration. We set them up and then begin leading their *imagination*, suggesting stuckness and associated qualities. As a result of the ideomotor effect, their muscles respond and create the effect in *physiology*. This creates the platform for the overall *experience* which, in turn, feeds back into the belief that hypnosis is happening and that this specific experience is occurring as a result, which feeds forward into further imaginative engagement... and so on and so forth.

Belief drives imagination, which modifies physiology, to create an experience that confirms/reinforces belief.

Essentially, in facilitating a hypnotic experience, we are aiming to get our co-operator into a loop and keep them in it long enough for it to become self-perpetuating. Once you have someone in a self-perpetuating loop, you can back off a little and give them more space because the loop is now running itself.

This example is somewhat simplified (in reality there are loops within loops) but, without diving too deep too fast, can you already see how this model could be useful to us as hypnotists?

Firstly, once you are aware of the looping nature of the process, and the importance of feedback, you can structure suggestions that play directly to it. You can also cultivate greater awareness of when the loop starts to self-perpetuate. This helps you choose the right time to challenge, which in turn reinforces the loop. You might also become aware of the point at which a co-operator might be 'popping out' of a loop, which helps you to focus your trouble shooting.

More fundamentally, the loop model offers us four points through which we can enter or influence the loop. Although *belief* is the primary driver, we don't always have to enter at that point. We could begin with *imagination*, or by setting *physiological* conditions (positioning the body etc.) or pace what's happening in the co-operator's current *experience* (we haven't discussed 'pacing' yet but we'll get to it). Through this awareness we can guide the loops toward the outcomes we (ourselves and our co-operator) desire, ensuring we pay attention to all the elements.

Back in the days when I was conducting a lot of street hypnosis experiments, as it became clear to me that the 'trance model' had serious flaws, I came to regard the hypnotic loop as the fundamental engine of hypnosis. In my view, not only do all hypnotic phenomena, including all the ideodynamic effects I've just mentioned, arise from hypnotic loops, but so too does all human experience. When I first started thinking about hypnosis in this way, I almost immediately became more effective at both facilitating hypnotic experiences and helping people free themselves from repeated unwanted experiences in their lives. I hope you will experience a similar benefit in making use of this loop model.

In every hypnosis session, I'm constantly setting up and monitoring loops, and watching for the points at which they perpetuate themselves. When a loop seems to be running well, I'm always aware of where I can intervene to break it, or otherwise transition into a different loop entirely. Sometimes, I choose to leave one loop running while opening a second loop on top of the first. I have all kinds of ways of thinking about loops and applying them in my work so this is far from just a theoretical model — it's something that has a clear and practical impact on what I do as a practising hypnotist.

It is also important to realise that people are *always* running one kind of hypnotic loop or another, because they are essentially *always* generating their ongoing experience in this way. Even the person who says "I can't be hypnotised" and resolutely beds in to that position is actually running a hypnotic loop — the 'trance' of 'I Can't Be Hypnotised'! When you realise this, it becomes clear that the old idea of 'putting someone into/under hypnosis' misses something fairly major: that we are essentially *always* in one kind of 'hypnotic' reality (to use the term with some licence) or another. Knowing this, the craft becomes one of shifting people from the loops they are in to new co-created loops that are going to delight, amuse or serve them in some practical way.

Keep this idea of the hypnotic loop in mind throughout the rest of this book and beyond. It may be a very simple model but it's also a very powerful one.

Hypnotic Focus

Hypnotic focus is an *uncritical* focus on current and anticipated experience. When a person is hypnotically focused they are totally and uncritically absorbed in the moment. Some have suggested to me that this is essentially the same as 'hypnotic trance' but hypnotic focus has nothing whatsoever to do with a particular state, depth or increased suggestibility.

If we think about the nature of hypnosis, it's not hard to see why this notion of hypnotic focus is tremendously important. Hypnosis involves establishing new hypnotic loops within a person's mind-body. Although our aim is to take people into these new loops, many factors within a co-operator's mind or environment could easily 'pop them out' or stop them forming a loop in the first place. One of the commonest is an actively critical or sceptical stance. If the co-operator's attitude is, "This is ridiculous, there's no way this is going to work", you are not going to be able to directly create an effective hypnotic loop (although they are in fact already in one of their own that both stabilises and is stabilised by their current sceptical reality).

This being the case, a major part of establishing good hypnotic focus concerns de-potentiating critical thinking on the part of our co-operator, clearing the way for absolute absorption in the unfolding experience you are facilitating. This is quite distinct from the classic idea of a 'trance' state where getting the hypnotee more 'deeply' under hypnotic influence is the main aim. Eschewing notions of depth, hypnotic focus is more usefully thought of as a simple binary situation: the co-operator either achieves hypnotic focus (including suspension of their critical faculty) or they don't.

Sometimes you'll find your co-operator is having difficulty focusing because there are too many environmental distractions. I'm not suggesting you need absolute peace and quiet to effectively facilitate hypnosis (I have done much hypnosis in noisy pubs over the years), but you *do* need your co-operator to be able to achieve hypnotic focus.

Here's a story that illustrates what I mean. On one occasion I was attempting to facilitate some hypnotic experiences with the landlord of a busy town pub. He had requested this out of his own curiosity and so was entirely willing to participate but it was clear as we began the process that he had a lot on his mind. Being the landlord of the establishment he was, of course, concerned with everything that was going on in the pub: people coming and going, how well his staff were doing their jobs, the customers, the atmosphere and so on. There were so many distractions that he simply couldn't focus enough to allow himself to be drawn into the hypnotic loop. We didn't achieve the required hypnotic focus and he didn't experience an interesting altered reality. Later that evening, when things has quietened down a little, the landlord got one of his staff to take over the pub for ten minutes. Having done this, he was able to clear his mind of previous concerns, achieve focus, shift into the hypnotic loops that I was facilitating and have some very interesting experiences as a result.

Sometimes the issue is less environmental and more cognitive: an overactive critical faculty! You might find yourself dealing with someone who has a generally sceptical outlook, or is specifically sceptical about hypnosis or your hypnotic abilities. Whatever the origin, when people are caught up in critical thinking they tend to have a lot of internal dialogue going on. This dialogue constantly evaluates and analysing their experience. This presents a challenge in drawing such people into new hypnotic loops because their critical thinking comes from and therefore maintains their current reality and beliefs. This is not to say they *cannot* experience hypnosis, only that the won't so long as they maintain their current position. You need to be fairly skilled as a hypnotist and facilitator to quieten their critical faculty and encourage the hypnotic focus that will enable them to have the experience they want *by suggestion alone*. Sometimes, however, this problem can be easily remedied by a frank conversation and a little coaching (we'll talk more about this later).

To sum up, hypnotic focus is a state of complete and uncritical absorption in the present moment, including all that you are suggesting and the resultant experience they are having. It is not in any sense a 'trance' and doesn't involve the notion of 'depth' in the traditional sense (although people could be more or less 'absorbed' in what is manifesting).

Frames and Framing

We've already looked at the notion of mental maps. The map metaphor is linked to another concept called *framing*. As we discuss framing here, please be aware that this presentation is a huge simplification and the actual mental processes involved are a lot more subtle and nuanced!

To understand framing, imagine that as you go about your life, in each and every moment, you are constantly asking yourself this question:

"*What is it that is happening here?*"

To answer this question, you refer to your mental map. The answer you come up with is the *frame* you put around the situation you're in and the events that you're experiencing. Imagine you were unexpectedly teleported, 'Star Trek' style, to a different location and situation and found yourself running around a field kicking a ball, with a number of other people chasing around after the same ball. At an unconscious level, you would immediately ask yourself, "What's happening here?"

Putting aside the weirdness of being transported in such a way, your answer might be, "I'm playing football" (or 'soccer' if you are on that side of the pond).

Your unconscious answer frames the moment and so makes sense of what you're seeing and experiencing. On top of this initial frame, you might layer in other frames, such as, "This is a very important competition", "This game is just a bit of casual fun between friends" , or, "I hate football."

Different people taking part in the same activity will put different combinations of frames around it, thereby creating different experiences for themselves. One player might seem very aggressive and competitive because they have applied a frame that says, "This is a deadly important competition and I'm determined to win". Another might apply a frame of, "Just a bit of fun".

Earlier, we looked at the idea of the hypnotic partnership. This is a frame in itself. It answers the question, "What is happening here?" with, "It's a partnership".

The concept of framing applies to hypnosis in two important ways.

First of all, the frames that *you* apply to what you're doing *within your own mind* will always influence the unfolding of events within the session and, therefore, the results that emerge. This is because you can *only* act and respond from within the frames through which you yourself are making sense. Understanding this, it is clear that some frames are going to be more useful than others.

For example, if you unconsciously view hypnosis as a zero sum game in which you are out to outsmart your co-operator and dominate their mind, this will not only shape your choices in the moment but will also shape your attitude. However much you try to hide it, you *will* communicate this reality to the co-operator and recruit them into it. The hypnotist operating out of this frame creates a counterproductive 'battle of wills' that might otherwise not have been there (way to reduce influence!). I sometimes call this 'the picnic principle':

Be careful what you take to the picnic because that may very well be what you end up eating.

The 'operator-side' frames that I offer in this book are all tried, tested and proven to be useful in terms of getting good hypnotic results. There's nothing, however, to stop you exploring and experimenting with other frames and frameworks. Indeed, once you have developed some proficiency with hypnosis, I would strongly encourage you to do so. As you're aware by now, one frame that I personally don't use is the 'trance' frame. This doesn't mean you can't experiment with it if you feel drawn to do so. Just remember, your frames and sensemaking count, because hypnosis starts from the inside out. You can only communicate and influence from where you are at, and where you are at will to a great extent be conveyed to your co-operator via your tonality, body posture, facial expressions, word choices, linguistic presuppositions and more. Be careful what you take to that picnic!

The second way that framing is relevant to the practise of hypnosis concerns the explicit frames you offer your co-operators. Our aim with these frames is to help them make sense of things in terms of both shaping their engagement with the process and creating the possibility (or even likelihood) of the desired results manifesting. Some frames will help your co-operator while others will hinder or even completely prevent them from successfully experiencing the shifts you are looking to facilitate.

For example, consider someone who comes to the hypnotic interaction with the frame: "Hypnosis only works on weak minded and gullible people." If hypnotic shifts started to happen, their answer to, "What's happening here?" would be something like, "I am being weak and allowing my mind to be controlled." If this runs counter to their personal values (as it would for most), it's unlikely they would allow themselves to engage any further with the process, instead running cognitions that work against the formation of new hypnotic loops. Similarly, if someone frames hypnosis as 'bad and scary', this is also going to hinder the process.

You can see from this example why effective pre-framing for the co-operator is such an important part of our work as hypnotists. It is essential that we establish useful frames at the front end of the process so that when they inwardly ask, "What's happening here?" as the process unfolds, they come up with an answer that motivates them to continue or even increase their engagement. In short, the quality of the framing of the session, both in advance and while it's in progress, is a major factor in its success.

Beyond the facilitation work itself, understanding frames and framing is of huge importance in all changework (hypnotic or otherwise). If a client leaves a session making exactly the same sense of their situation and what's possible for them as when they came in, there will be no change. When they leave seeing things differently (and therefore running different hypnotic loops) they will experience things differently and have access to new resultant behaviours. This kind of work is way beyond the scope of this book but is the focus of level 3 of my HWT Online Deep Apprenticeship.

This has only been a brief introduction to frames and framing. Later in the book we will look at the practical aspects of framing for both engagement and results in hypnosis. Beyond hypnosis, understanding frames and framing will enrich every aspect of your life because it will enable you to 'see the matrix'. That is, 'see' how people are organising their reality in fundamental ways. The resultant ability to utilise, set and manipulate frames will significantly increase your efficacy and influence as a communicator (professional or otherwise).

If you'd like to study this subject in far greater detail, the seminal text is 'Frame Analysis' by Irving Goffman.

Plausibility

Before we conclude this introductory chapter and get into the practicalities of conducting a hypnosis session, I want to discuss the notion of *plausibility*. As hypnotists, we're aiming to engage our co-operators in a process that will shift their experience of reality. However, people will only manifest shifts in reality that seem *plausible* within their belief system (or internal map of reality) and their current framing of 'this moment'. Please bear in mind as we explore this that the *plausibility* we are talking about is not an *intellectual* thing, but a much deeper, *felt* thing.

Let me start this section by describing a situation that I (and, no doubt, many others) have encountered many times: working with my co-operator, I successfully facilitate an experience that would classically be considered a 'deep trance' phenomenon. Flowing forward from this initial success, I begin opening up a loop for another phenomenon that ought to be *simpler* (requiring less 'depth' by traditional standards) but it just isn't catching so easily. This is by no means uncommon and was in fact one of the major spurs to my initial questioning of the trance model .

So, how can we explain such occasions when the 'harder' phenomena unfold easily but the 'easier' ones don't? Providing you've set up the loops well, drawn your co-operator into the experience and engendered the hypnotic focus, I think it mostly comes down to plausibility (though there may be other variables in the mix too, such as individual cognitive proclivities). All else being equal, plausibility is the major difference maker.

If the person you are working with regards a given phenomenon as plausible (in terms of their mental map, their beliefs and their frame around the current situation), and *if* you've successfully established the loop, the phenomenon will manifest (assuming it is humanly possible). If, however, it *doesn't* seem plausible, they will simply pop out of the loop. Essentially, as soon as what you are suggesting violates your co-operator's rules of reality, your loop work will completely unravel. This being so, effective hypnotists must know how to engender plausibility and avoid triggering the incredulity (however mild) that can destroy the loops we wish to nurture. We need to attend to this *both* in our overall framing *and* in the specifics of our suggestion work.

As an example of the latter, let's say I'm demonstrating to someone the 'power of their mind' (this is the frame) by facilitating the experience of having their hand apparently stick to something. In the suggestion work for this effect, I will not only talk about the hand 'sticking' but *also* suggest their *arm* 'locking'. Why? Because some people don't find the idea of their hand sticking to something very plausible (why would it?) but can easily manifest a locking phenomenon through the experience of rigidity in their muscles, fingers or hands. The concept of 'locking' is simply more plausible to them than the idea of 'sticking'. Knowing this, I always mention *both* terms, sticking and locking, which are both paths to the same result. Of course, some might regard sticking as more plausible than locking (people make up their reality just the way that they do!)

You can never know in advance of a session what people will find plausible or otherwise (though with experience, your guesses will become more 'educated'). You might work with someone who finds the concept of their name disappearing from their mind more plausible than their hand sticking to a table or their arm becoming rigid (even though, in classical terms, amnesia is supposed to be a 'deeper' trance phenomenon than catalepsy). Because you don't always know ahead of time what your co-operator will find sufficiently plausible, it pays to develop multiple options and to always be attending to feedback so as you can change tack when you need to. This kind of manoeuvrability is a key element of the HWT approach.

Please note that plausibility is *not* a binary condition — things can be *more* or *less* plausible. Interestingly, although we require a sufficient level of plausibility for something to manifest, once we have crossed that threshold the experiences that have *lower* levels of plausibility will tend to have the *highest* impact for our co-operators.

In the Introduction I mentioned that I've prepared a booklet containing transcripts of hypnosis sessions. You can get this free of charge from my website: www.hypnosiswithouttrance.com/transcripts

One of the transcripts is called 'Hypnotherapy Office'. During this session, I facilitated for my co-operator a block in accessing his name (hypnotic name amnesia) and the experience of being unable to see me whilst looking at me (negative visual hallucination). I thought 'invisibility' would feel *more* impressive than a small bit of temporary amnesia. However, when I asked for feedback, my co-operator said he was more impressed by the name amnesia than anything else. Why? Because whilst I had engineered enough plausibility to get both effects, he found the amnesia *less* plausible than the negative hallucination. It was more of a stretch for his imagination and his understanding of the world that he should be separated, even temporarily, from something that was so much a part of who he was. You can never make safe assumptions about other people's maps, models of reality and what they will, or will not, consider plausible.

That said, you can make *educated guesses* about plausibility and it's generally a good idea to do so. This brings us to the notion of the 'hypnotic ladder', which we'll look at in more detail in the section on transitioning between hypnotic loops.

When working hypnotically, it's best to start from phenomena that your co-operator is likely to consider highly plausible and then progressively step up through experiences that they might normally consider less and less plausible. Each successful result feeds back into the co-operator's beliefs concerning the power of the work, creating a frame wherein the seemingly less plausible phenomena start to feel within the realm of possibility.

For example, someone who hasn't experienced 'the power of hypnosis' might find the idea of being unable to see someone standing in front of them ridiculous. However, once they have experienced several phenomena outside their rules for everyday reality, the idea of invisibility begins to seem less far-fetched. With each successive experience you create a rung on a hypnotic ladder that climbs towards the ultimate outcome: the perception of invisibility.

Plausibility, Framing and 'The Big Because'

We've talked individually about *belief systems*, *framing* and *plausibility*, but it is how these three areas interconnect that is of major importance to us as hypnotists. Why? Because:

> We need to lay frames that fit well enough with our co-operators' maps of the world to engender 'buy in' for the overall process, while also creating a context of plausibility for the phenomena we wish to evoke.

Put another way, we want to connect our co-operators with an understanding that has them *both* engage with the process fully *and* accept the weird things that are going to happen as entirely plausible (given the circumstances).

One of the major advantages of formal hypnosis over covert hypnosis is that it allows us to explicitly set frames. In both forms of hypnotic work we are always framing and re-framing as we go, but in formal hypnosis the explicitness with which we are able to do this allows us a far greater scope to select frames that we can leverage for stronger phenomena. This explicit setting of frames at the beginning of the session is called *pre-framing*, and its primary aim is to provide what might be thought of as the 'big because' upon which the whole session is founded.

In HWT the 'big because' is the central, plausible, overarching reason *why* the weird distortions of reality you intend to evoke are actually possible and, ideally, fairly inevitable, as a result of engagement with the process. This is absolutely key: going back to Wilson's notions of the 'Thinker' and the 'Prover', if your co-operator considers something to be impossible, their Prover will find ways to prove that this is the case. Conversely, if they think a given phenomenon is inevitable, their Prover will get to work creating results that prove this to be so.

Looking at it like this, a big because can be *anything* that provides a plausible reason for the desired effects according to the co-operator's map of the world. And when I say 'anything', I do mean anything:

- Because the hypnotist has magic powers.
- Because of chi energy.
- Because we are bringing different brain systems online.
- Because of the power of the Hermes.
- Because of voodoo.
- Because of a special state of mind.

From a technical perspective (though not necessarily an ethical one), your choice of 'big because' is not overly important, *providing* it is sufficiently plausible to your co-operator in terms of their 'map of the world' *and* provides a compelling explanatory frame for the effects you wish to create. However, you should always consider how your framing may impact your co-operator's life after the session! For example, whilst some people might resist a 'mind control' frame, others might buy into it readily. If the cooperator *does* buy into it, this frame could be an effective way to create some interesting phenomena during the session. However, consider the potentially negative implications of that person believing they are controllable in this way. Would that be empowering for them?

As a simple rule, always set frames that, in addition to their utility in the session, are likely to enrich your co-operator's experience of themselves and their lives going forward, and avoid those that could foreseeably be to their detriment.

With this consideration in mind, our aim with pre-conversation is to set the frame for the entire hypnotic interaction that follows. Aside from providing a plausible explanatory context for the desired phenomena, our primary aim in pre-conversation is to create 'buy-in' for overall engagement with the process. Buy-in here engenders the co-operation required for formal hypnosis to take place; without it we have no dance partner to dance with. The buy-in we need operates on two levels:

1. Buy-in for the overall process ('hypnosis' or whatever you are stating you do).
2. Buy-in to *you* as the operator — that is, belief in your skills and competence.

Yes, you too need to be considered plausible as a facilitator of the work! It is not enough that someone resonates with your 'big because' if they ultimately don't also believe in *you*. It is therefore important that you are solid in your own understandings of hypnosis and how it works, even if you are to translate those into different frames for your co-operator. Remember this:

People buy what's solid!

Bring your insecurities and this will undermine your co-operators' perceptions of you. Bring a solid understanding of your craft and what you are about and this will create buy-in for *you*. This doesn't mean you need to be seen as an expert or that you need to fake anything. Just be grounded and certain in who you are and what you are doing, even if your role is that of an explorer just starting to discover what might be possible via hypnosis.

So, getting down to the craft of it: I'm hoping that it goes without saying that establishing a big because through pre-conversation is *not* simply a matter of blurting out a line like, *"Hypnosis works because of the power of your mind"* and then moving on. You *will* want to have an *interactive conversation*. This means being able and ready to answer your client's questions about your chosen frame in a way that they find credible. It will be of great help to have useful analogies to deploy as and when needed as part of the process. It may also help to be able to draw useful diagrams if needed. When you learn to set up your big because with subtlety and finesse (though these are not always necessary), you will be well on your way to becoming an excellent hypnotist. Without this skill you will — regrettably — be close to nowhere! We will be getting further into the craft of pre-framing later in this book. For now, simply think of yourself as an educator, helping this person to better understand something that will be of benefit to them, regardless of whether they go ahead to dance the hypnotic dance with you. Frame this as a gift for them rather than as a means to an end for you.

Before we move on, I would like to look at how the idea of the 'big because' applies in both overt and covert hypnosis respectively, as it is the major element that shapes respective strengths and weaknesses of both.

With overt hypnosis, people know that they are going to be engaging in some formal process (be it framed as 'hypnosis', 'energy work', a ' psychological experiment' or whatever). For this reason we can *explicitly* and *co-operatively* set a 'big because' that is generative of strong hypnotic outcomes (shifts that take our co-operator a long way from their everyday reality). For example, an hallucination can happen *because* [insert powerful and plausible frame of choice] is *understood* to be happening. This ability to take people a long way out of their everyday experience is the particular strength of overt hypnosis. This great strength, however, is equally the foundation for its greatest weakness: because the framing is so explicit, it's easy for someone to either reject the frame outright or, for whatever reason, to simply reject engagement with the overall process.

With covert hypnosis (which, as already stated, is *not* what this book is about) the situation is quite different. Since you're using your skills and understandings 'under the radar' — covertly and conversationally — your hypnotee is entirely unaware of the unfolding process. There is no big because being offered (and what isn't offered cannot be rejected) and no *explicit* process to opt out of. When working covertly, we use our language and communication to strategically pull the person we are communicating with into processing that aligns with our intention, but in no way strikes them as unusual. This is the strength of covert hypnosis: it's 'under the radar' and so there is less to consciously reject. However, because the frame put around the interaction is one of a normal, everyday conversation, there is nothing to leverage for the purpose of getting the 'out of the ordinary' to happen. The rule here is: any effect outside the realm of everyday experience, such as a hand sticking to something or a person turning invisible, requires a 'big because' that will take the hypnotee into a 'realm' where such things can happen. Nothing will happen that isn't congruent with the frame in play (such as 'business meeting' or 'chat with a friend') regardless of the hypnotic skills you might deploy. For this reason, getting 'far out' responses with covert hypnosis is going to be challenging in the extreme. I won't say it's impossible, because I don't like that word, but it is certainly something I have never seen demonstrated in my many years mixing with the best in this field.

What you *can* readily achieve with covert hypnosis are effects that fall within the range of typical everyday experience, because they *do not* challenge the implicit frame in any way. For example, we all experience shifts in our *emotional* state as a matter of course. As there is nothing implausible about such shifts occurring within the frame of everyday conversation, they can be covertly facilitated via the conversational application of hypnosis principles and skills. In my professional coaching work, I predominantly use hypnotic principles and skills to facilitate mind-shifts entirely within the context of coaching dialogue. Whilst some clients know me as a hypnotist (so the frame may be implicitly in play) many do not. When adeptly employed, covert hypnosis can be can be just as powerful as overt hypnosis (if not more so) as a means for helping people change their lives. It is worth noting, however, that although there's no big because for the process overall, there will be subtler 'becauses' seeded within the process for the purpose of driving changes.

To sum up, with overt hypnosis you can achieve more out of the ordinary effects, because you are able to leverage explicit frames that allow for them, but also risk evoking scepticism through the rejection of those frames. With covert hypnosis, there's no scepticism regarding the frame because the framing is implicit and commonplace rather than explicit and unusual, but you will be limited to more commonplace phenomena as a result. Always bear this in mind: the more unusual the phenomenon you want to manifest, the more work you have to do to create the necessary, highly plausible frames.

2

THE HYPNOTIC

PROCESS

2. The Hypnotic Process

In the last chapter, we looked at the definitions and principles underpinning Hypnosis Without Trance. Let's now shift to more practical considerations. In this chapter we are going to proceed, step by step, through the 'how to' of conducting a complete, formal hypnosis session, geared towards evoking phenomena. Note this is not a changework session, which would have more complexity to it.

Please be aware that this chapter is densely packed with many nuanced details. It is primarily intended to be something of a 'manual' that you can return to again and again as you explore and practise, rather than a simple 'top level' explanation. If there is anything that doesn't make full sense as you initially read it, that's okay; it will become clearer and more relevant the more you progress on your *practical* learning journey with Hypnosis Without Trance. And speaking of this learning journey...

The Magic Key to Learning

Throughout this book, I'm going to share a great deal of practical material with you. This presents you with two options. Your first option is to sit around *thinking* about all of this information and wondering if or how it would work in practice. Your second option is to go out and find someone to practise with, experiment, learn-by-doing and thereby develop your hypnotic skills. I *strongly* encourage you to take the second option. It's the only one that works.

For many years, I had a purely academic interest in hypnosis, NLP and psychology. I read deeply into these topics but never actually tried to apply what I knew in real life. In all honesty, I was afraid that if I tried something — such as a simple hypnotic induction — I might fail, which would mean I was a failure. This fear of failure stopped me even *trying* to succeed.

This all changed due to to an experience I had when training formally in NLP. I'd read extensively on the subject before the first course (Practitioner level) and so picked everything up fairly quickly during the live training. All this pre-learning made me somewhat the 'star' of the course, which of course was all good for pumping up my ego (which perhaps needed it at the time).

Because I loved the training and what I had learnt so much, I enrolled on the Master Practitioner course set to run just a couple of months later. I was not the only one from my practitioner cohort to go on to do the master practitioner: Sarah was there too. On the practitioner course Sarah, although keen, had been a little shaky in her facilitation work to say the least. However, when she showed up on the Master Practitioner training she was like a woman transformed. Her facilitation was now crisp, clear and confidently executed and certainly left me in the shade. I was quite blown away by the change,so I had to know how she had achieved this remarkable improvement. When I asked her she gave me a very simple answer: she said she had been out *practising with people*. Real, live people! This was her 'secret sauce'. I, in contrast, had practised with virtually no-one. Though I loved what I had learned on the first course and had enjoyed talking about all the theory and techniques, I'd tried out very little of it in real life. I realised what ought to have been obvious from the start: if I wanted to develop significant NLP facilitation skills, I needed to actually practise the NLP processes with real, live human beings.

What *was* clear, was that something was holding me back from practising. When I felt into this a little it became clear that I was unconsciously concerned that in trying this NLP stuff for real, I might somehow reveal my shortcomings — I might find that I just wasn't that good. Reflecting upon this a little more deeply, it struck me that this is precisely what practice is for! The *point* of practising is to discover your strengths and weaknesses; to see where you're already fairly good and where you need to improve. From that point forward, I adopted a new policy of taking every conceivable opportunity to practise hypnosis and NLP, which sometimes meant 'feeling the fear and doing it anyway' (as Susan Jeffers suggests in her very popular book *Feel the Fear and Do It Anyway*). Formal or informal settings, street or bar, anywhere and everywhere. I tried out all the hypnotic techniques I knew and did my best to learn from every single experience — whether I got great results or none.

So I entreat you; don't make the same initial mistake that I made. Don't let fear cheat you out of developing real expertise. Get up, go out and explore hypnosis with real people in real life (or, at least, Skype or Zoom!).

As a matter of definition, you cannot gain practical skills by studying theory in abstract. You cannot develop real-world skills by sitting around thinking and reading books. This is not to say that good information isn't valuable, only that in order to work up real skills you have to take the information and explore with it in actual practice. So, find people to do hypnosis with, experiment and learn by trial and error. You will fail from time to time (maybe even a lot at first) but such is the nature of things; there is no real learning without failure. Taking this kind of action will turn *information* into *transformation*.

One option to liberate yourself from the tyranny of fearing failure is to adopt the attitude 'there is no failure, only *feedback*'. Indeed, if you are wishing to progress in this craft, the only true failure would be taking no action in the first place.

Another option is to take ownership of failure as the beautiful, generative thing that it can be. Beautiful? Generative? Yes! Because it is only when we are making mistakes that we are meeting the boundaries of current patterning, which we *must* meet in order to move beyond them. This is why making mistakes is absolutely essential if you wish to learn. As legendary impro theatre coach Keith Johnstone used to say, "Not progressing? Well, you just don't love failure enough!" Whichever way of making sense of this works best for you, please don't let fear of making mistakes stop you from going out and practising all that you learn from this book. So, going beyond fear, who should you practise with?

You may initially be inclined, as many people are, to start by practising with family and friends. Although most convenient, this is often *not* the best place to start. Why not? Because of their existing beliefs about who and what you are. They will see you as a brother/sister, old friend (et cetera) and *not* as someone who has skills or knowledge with hypnosis, and this can create a barrier.

If you are going to work with people who know you, the best way to get round this barrier is to avoid claiming that you're doing any kind of hypnosis at all. Instead, you can just say that you've been learning a lot of interesting things about how the mind works, and ask them if they would like to help you conduct a brief experiment in mind-body connection (you could mention the ideomotor principle and give a little historical detail). You let them know that all they need to do is follow your instructions 100%, complete each step of the experiment and really pay attention to what they notice happening. Do emphasise that you want them to let you know exactly what it was like and how it felt, so as to encourage them to focus in and engage more.

In the previous chapter we discussed the concept of framing; here we have stepped away from a strong 'hypnosis' frame (although we are still seeding the idea a little by mentioning it as a related phenomenon) and replacing it with an 'experiment' frame. The person you're practising with is part of the experiment and all they have to do, whatever happens or doesn't happen, is to let you know exactly what it was like for them.

Note also with this framing that there can be no failure. An experiment aims to find out information, not achieve a specific outcome. Whatever happens, so long as you get honest feedback from your practice partner you have success (and really do aim to learn from the feedback you receive). The main skill to work on within this frame is that of engendering full and sincere engagement in the experiment on the part of your practise partner.

If you are having difficulty finding cooperative people to practice with, the Hypnosis Without Trance Online Deep Apprenticeship (details at HypnosisWithoutTrance.com) provides ample opportunities to practise via the online community group.

The Hypnosis Without Trance Process

The process we are going to unpack here consists of five stages. Just to be clear, these stages provide a 'roadmap in abstract' that will help you to learn the Hypnosis Without Trance process. However, they are not intended to be strictly or rigidly adhered to during a real session. When you're hypnotically facilitating for real, the session will flow from start to finish in an apparently seamless way, and aspects from the different stages will inevitably overlap.

The five stages are:

1. Set-up and pre-framing
2. Managing buy-in and establishing hypnotic focus
3. Generating, testing and managing the loops
4. Closing the final loop and handing back control.
5. Crediting and empowering

Let's look at each of these in detail.

Stage 1: Set-Up and Pre-Framing

In this first stage, our aim is to uncover the co-operator's beliefs about hypnosis and work with them to create a platform of understandings that allow us to do effective hypnotic work. Assuming your prospective co-operator has heard of hypnosis, they will already have some ideas about it (ones that sit congruently within their broader worldview). These ideas create a *frame* that may or may not be useful to us, so it's best to start by ascertaing what they are. Once we understand the co-operator's frame, we can work to utilise it, adapt it or (if necessary) replace it, to create complete 'buy in' for the ensuing process.

This is really important. If you're going to do overt hypnosis with someone, they need to *desire* to do it with total commitment. You do *not* want to be drawn into a battle of wills or anything similar as this will only work against you.

Why is this stage is so important? After all, could we not just dive straight in with an attempted elicitation of the desired phenomena? You may have seen some hypnotists apparently doing just this on YouTube. Perhaps the hypnotist starts with a handshake interrupt 'induction' and then goes straight into some kind of hypnotic phenomenon.

There's no doubt that this is possible (I admit I have done similar things myself on limited occasions). However, what you *don't* see on YouTube are all the times this doesn't work — and I can assure you it fails far more often than it succeeds. If your aim is to optimise the success of your facilitations, you will want to include this set-up and pre-framing stage and take appropriate time doing it. Done well, the set up and pre-frame *will* do most of the 'heavy lifting' for you.

This stage is so important because, as we've seen, hypnosis is primarily about the engagement of beliefs, and this stage is where this work begins. We have already looked at the importance of beliefs and framing in the first chapter. At this stage, our aim is to help our co-operator make meaning around what is about to happen, in such a way as to:

- Give a plausible explanation ('big because') for why the phenomena we intend to evoke are possible and even inevitable under certain conditions.

- Engender 'buy-in' for the process by stimulating curiosity and engaging any other useful motivation, in conjunction with the plausibility of the frame.

- Establish you as enough of an authority in this domain to be successfully facilitating this experience (this is more about non-verbal elements — how you 'carry yourself' in the exchange - than about giving a résumé).

Remember from the last chapter our discussion of plausibility and the 'big because'? This stage is where these key ideas primarily come into play. The person you are about to work with *must* find what you're going to do to be completely plausible, so your job here is to 'sell' it to them in a way that fits with their map of reality. Our major aim here is the establishment of a 'big because' that sells the whole game: a key, central idea that explains *why* what is about to happen is possible (and, ideally, inevitable under the conditions you will be setting up).

To repeat for emphasis: people don't buy into anything without a rationale — something that makes complete sense to them. When you are hypnotically facilitating someone you are altering their perceived reality — an alteration that is driven by *belief itself* (hence 'beliefs' occupying the top position in the Hypnotic Loop). At this stage we are essentially co-creating, through our pre-conversation, a credible 'why' that will provide a foundation for the entire process and all the phenomena that emerge from it. This is our 'big because'.

For example, a person's hand isn't going to stick to something for no reason at all. They aren't going to see something that isn't there unless there's a reason that allows for this to happen. In formal hypnosis, the big because is *usually* the concept of hypnosis itself: the co-operator finds it plausible that their hand is stuck because they are 'in hypnosis'. Our big because is the frame that engenders every aspect of the hypnotic experience, from engagement to results.

However, an explicit 'hypnosis frame' isn't the only option here. As one alternative, I often use the frame of 'energy work'. The concept of 'chi' is central to the worldview underpinning the Chinese 'internal' martial and healing arts (which I have studied and practised for many years). As this is part of my background I sometimes use this as my big because when working with ideomotor phenomena such as sticking or arm levitation. My framing here might be that we are working with the deeper processes that the Taoist alchemists make sense of in terms of 'chi'. Note that I am not making any hard claim that chi is absolutely real. This is to give the frame some malleability in terms of how it might fit with the co-operators worldview, as well as leave room for manoeuvre within the frame. If this frame resonates with the co-operator (for example if they have previously engaged successfully with some energy work) this can serve as a very credible big because.

Another big because I might use is simply 'the power of the mind'. When I was a magician (specialising in 'mentalism' or magic of the mind) I often presented routines framed this way because the idea that our minds have hidden capabilities is endemic in the culture I work within. Again, it has enough ambiguity to be malleable and adaptive. When working with this idea, especially if demonstrating apparently 'magical' effects, I wouldn't necessarily mention hypnosis even if I was only using Hypnosis Without Trance principles. 'The power of the mind' can be a sufficient big because to support all manner of hypnotic effects, from hands sticking to tables to seeing what isn't there... *provided that the person you are working with buys in!*

In reality, given enough creative thought, there are probably a near-infinite number of ways to effectively frame for hypnosis. So, just think: how many ways could I sell this game? And then refine your answers by asking yourself: what are all the implications of this framing? This is a highly recommended exercise!

Let's shift gears and get down to the practicalities. Note that in the following section we are going to assume that 'hypnosis' itself is our big because. For clarity, we will break 'Set-up And Pre-Framing' into three steps:

- Introduce hypnosis.
- Elicit the prospective co-operator's attitude.
- Choose an appropriate frame.

Introduce Hypnosis

This first step relates primarily to impromptu hypnosis demonstrations (including street hypnosis). If you are a hypnotherapist who never intends to work impromptu, you can skip this bit (unless you are curious about the psychology of it) as, in your case, hypnosis has already been introduced by your marketing and professional framing. People come to see you *because* you're a hypnotherapist so there's no need to introduce the idea of hypnosis in the session. However, when it comes to impromptu hypnosis the first task of 'set-up and pre-framing' is, of course, to introduce the topic of hypnosis into the conversation to create a context for potential demonstration.

There are many possible ways to do this. Before we get into specifics, I suggest that, if you intend to become a career hypnotist, you would be wise to harness the power of *legend* by pro-actively creating your reputation at every appropriate opportunity. Find ways to let people *know* that you have skills and knowledge in the field of hypnosis! When people ask you what you do, *say* you're a hypnotist (or practitioner of hypnosis or hypnotic facilitator) and tell them why you find the craft so fascinating. Never miss a chance to let people know that this is what you do, or at least something you study and have a keen interest in.

Do this as often as opportunity presents, seeding the idea of hypnosis among everyone you know and the people you meet (but do it with a little subtlety and *don't* be coming from a place of either lofty high-status or 'something to prove', as these attitudes are antagonistic rather than enrolling). Aim to get to the point where your reputation precedes you. If you do this, there will be times when you don't need to introduce the idea of hypnosis because the idea of hypnosis will introduce you! What I mean is that whenever your friends or people in your area happen to refer to hypnosis, your name will come up first.

In introducing the topic of hypnosis (assuming you are doing so to set the field for potential hypnotic work), do so in such a way as to trigger a sense of curiosity. One way to do this is to use the *curiosity hook*: instead of introducing hypnosis and then immediately starting to 'fire hose' your knowledge, mention it *in passing* and then deliberately say no more and wait for the people you're with to ask about it. Ideally, you want people chasing you for information and experience rather than you chasing them to participate, so bait the hook and let their curiosity bring them to you.

However, while it has great merit, the 'curiosity hook' is not appropriate for every situation. For example, if you're doing street hypnosis you usually need to adopt a much more direct approach: introduce yourself, mention hypnosis and get on with it!

Here's a little tip relating specifically to street hypnosis: select people who look like they're *not* especially 'on a mission'. So, for example, pubs are better than a busy thoroughfare because the people there generally intend to stick around to enjoy themselves. Avoid people who are plainly trying to get their errands done or get somewhere specific for a specific time. They likely won't have time to give you the time, let alone for you to do hypnosis. (If that seems obvious, I'm with you! But I have seen so many who are new to street hypnosis breaking this rule.)

If you are going to connect with new people with the express intention of facilitating hypnosis, be sure to do it as if it's the most natural thing in the world for you. Let it seem as though you've done it a million times, it's no big deal to you, you're used to it and people generally love it. Certainly don't approach people as if humbly asking for their permission. Be grounded in yourself and what you are doing: an experienced professional who does this kind of thing all the time, as a matter of course.

Back in my street hypnosis days, I never used a set script to connect with prospective co-operators I'd engage on the streets of London. However, my approach would generally be something along the following lines:

> "Hey, guys, how's it going? [await verbal and/or non verbal response] My name is James and... crazy as it is, I'm a hypnotist [brief pause] Ah, now I can see your reactions to that [assuming they have reacted]... why do people think that's odd [shrugging, playing it for a joke — there should be some laughs at this point if it's been played well]. Listen, I'm conducting some research today, just getting a sense of people's attitudes and understanding, so I'm not jumping into anyone's mind [again, played with levity]. Have you got a few moments for a conversation on this? Have any of you ever experienced hypnosis or anything like it?"

The aim here is to set up a dialogue, an interaction to draw people in, rather than deliver a stock pitch. Note that I pause to observe responses and take them into account. Also note the use of questions to encourage engagement. To really play this approach well, it helps to have a clipboard with some tick box (check box) questionnaires on it. In creating this, consider what you would genuinely be interested to know. Making the whole project as genuine as possible will make it more effective.

Elicit the Co-operator's Attitude

Having introduced the topic of hypnosis, the next step is to elicit the person's current beliefs and attitudes about it. Hypnosis exists as a 'cultural idea' so most people have beliefs and assumptions about it that will sometimes be useful and other times not so much. Remember that a major aim of our set up and pre-frame is getting 'buy-in'. We are selling our *big because* and selling ourselves as credible operators. Without knowing our potential co-operator's attitudes and beliefs we will be unable to align our 'sales pitch' (I use this metaphor with caution — make it a human conversation!) with their mental map of reality, thereby undermining our attempts to secure the requisite interest and buy-in.

For example, if somebody thinks hypnosis is about 'mind control', they may wish to avoid it or simply not believe that they could ever 'succumb' to it. This is not going to engender the kind of participation we require to work with them so we need to establish a different understanding.

So, how do we elicit their position? One easy opening is to simply ask, "Have you ever *experienced hypnosis* before?"

Consider the specific phrasing of this question. Note that it's distinct from, "Have you ever *been hypnotised* before?" Whereas the wording of the former subtly frames hypnosis as something that you do *with* your co-operator, the latter frames it as something that you do *to* a passive 'subject'. Our aim is to align with a spirit of partnership and co-operation, avoiding notions of a manipulative hypnotist and passive hypnotee. We require our co-operator to take an active role in the process and to follow instructions, not passively wait for 'the hypnosis' to take effect. Our aim is to engender an attitude of 'engage and create' rather than 'wait and see'. Invoking the frame of hypnosis as something you do *to* people may raise concerns that you are aiming to 'take control' of them in some way. (Whilst some people might actually want this, the vast majority do not).

By asking, "Have you ever experienced hypnosis before?" you are playing a different frame: you subtly convey the idea that hypnosis involves their *active participation*. This reduces the potential for perceived threat in your hypnotic interactions, which will always pay dividends in terms of quality of engagement and response. As this is a closed question, your co-operator will reply either 'yes' or 'no'.

> If they say yes, you ask, "What was that like for you, what happened?"

Listen attentively to what they tell you about their previous experience. If it was generally good, you can get some details about what the other hypnotist did and replicate some of those elements in your own facilitation (thus borrowing buy-in from the previous positive experience). You can also springboard off their positive experience by asking, "Would you be open to having a *really wonderful* experience of hypnosis?"

This subtly frames what you're going to do as being better than whatever they may have experienced previously. It's part of selling the experience to them. This is in alignment with the principle of WIIFM, which stands for, 'What's In It For Me?' When people are wondering whether to buy in to something, they're thinking, "What's in it for me?" Hence, suggesting that they can have a really wonderful experience, better than the one they had before, provides the WIIFM.

If the previous experience was negative, such as "I went to see this hypnotist but nothing worked", you still want to get the details so as to *avoid* doing anything that the previous hypnotist may have done. You also want to dispel any erroneous assumptions that the other hypnotist may have given the co-operator. For example, if they say, "He kept saying I would go deeper and deeper asleep, but I wasn't asleep at all", you might say, "I'm not surprised because hypnosis really has nothing to do with sleep. It's a shame that so many people claiming to know about the subject perpetuate such outdated and confused notions. Far from being about sleep, hypnosis is really about moving our minds in different ways, in order to create useful shifts in our experience" — or something along these lines.

> If they say no, you might ask, "What do you imagine it would be like to experience hypnosis?"

Here they have an opportunity to share their thoughts and fears. They may say something like, "Well, I don't know, I'm not sure it would work for me." If so, you might ask, "Well, if you could find out that it can work for you, would you be curious to do so?"

You are looking here for them to reply in the positive, but be careful to assess the person's tone and attitude. They might say, "Sure, why not" but more in a spirit of challenge than of cooperation, as if defying you to hypnotise them (though my wording of the question was chosen to avoid this, it is still possible). It's important to get really clear signs of co-operation at this point. You want to make sure they're not just playing around, testing your ability or challenging you to prove that hypnosis is real. You want to secure their cooperation and confirm their willingness to work with you to create an experience.

To be as sure as you can regarding the person's attitude, and whether or not they are going to be cooperative, *don't* just listen to what they say — also pay attention to how they *look* and their *tone of voice*. Do they seem nervous or scared that you might be about to hypnotise them? Do they seem cocky? If people look frightened, you will want to allay their fears. For example, you might say:

> "You know, a lot of people have funny ideas about hypnosis and I understand why. If you watch films and TV, you're going to get all kinds of weird ideas about mind control and the like. But, the truth is, hypnosis is really just about tapping into the deeper parts of your mind that are able to create intriguing and often valuable new experiences for you. New ways of being... new ways of seeing. New possibilities! This is why it's so useful for people looking to makes significant changes in their lives [WIIFM alert!]. I'm curious... if you were to find that you can move your mind in different ways... and create new possibilities for yourself... I wonder how you might apply that in your life?"

Note that this ends with a question. Whenever you ask such a question, listen attentively to the reply. Pay attention, make mental notes and look for clues that might signal cooperation or defiance. Many practitioners of hypnosis don't do this. Instead they rely on a set script that they deliver every time by rote (robot-style!). It's far better to open a conversation and listen carefully so you understand exactly how this person thinks and feels about hypnosis. This is the way to really engage them, build rapport and generate the most appropriate framing for them as the individual they are. This leads us on to the next section.

Select an Appropriate Frame

Once you have elicited your co-operators's attitude, you can select and adapt an appropriate frame for the work. The first 'inside secret' of effective framing for hypnosis is to remember that there is no consensus, even among 'experts', as to what hypnosis actually *is*. This means we are free to use any frame that enables us to get the engagement we want. The trick here is to find a frame that is a good fit for *both* your co-operator *and* yourself, because if you can't buy-in to the frame yourself, you'll do a poor job selling it to your co-operator. Here are some 'headlines' for some frames I might use (just capturing the essence — they'd be built on and developed in delivery).

Hypnosis is really just...

- The power of your mind to create shifts in experience.
- The bringing online of different brain-systems to create different outcomes.
- Applied neuroscience.
- Connecting with your deeper, unconscious programming to work with it in useful ways.
- Engaging your untapped ability to shift your immediate experience of this moment.
- A way of releasing yourself from stuck psychological patterns, so your mind can create different results.
- A kind of powerful, focused creative daydreaming that actually creates lasting differences in your mind and body.
- Connecting you into your untapped potential.
- Working with certain cognitive effects to create different outcomes.

You'll note that each of these frames has a *lot* of ambiguity built into them. The point is not so much what they say but how much they resonate for the client (plausibility again). That said, none of them are devoid of meaning. If the co-operator were to ask me questions about any of them, I would be able to say what I mean in more detailed terms. Essentially, I have a variety of ways of explaining hypnosis, each of which I understand and can explain, and I will let these inform me throughout my set up conversation (all the while monitoring for buy-in).

We have already looked at how we might frame hypnosis for someone who seems fearful or wary. If the person is still rather unsure despite your framing but is nonetheless showing signs of curiosity, one option is to deploy the 'not hypnosis' frame, which works like this:

> "Would you like to do something that will give you a sense of how powerful your own mind can be?"

> "Yes."

> "It's not really hypnosis... but it will give you a sense of how hypnosis works, yeah?"

What we are doing here is seeding the idea of hypnosis, whilst simultaneously taking it off the table and replacing it with something less threatening that also has greater 'useful ambiguity' to it. We are also dropping the sneaky presupposition that hypnosis is a legitimate thing that actually works (more on linguistic presupposition later). Note that 'tag question' at the end. When you say that final 'yeah?', you want to look at your co-operator and raise your eyebrows slightly to encourage agreement (a little acting skill goes a long way in hypnotic facilitation). You want to engender a feeling of agreement at this point, because this is what carries the buy-in you're looking for. Be monitoring for buy-in, and when you sense you are getting it ask:

"So you're up for doing this?!"

This question you express as if it were a *statement*. What you're actually doing here is delivering the question using what is called *command* tonality. We'll learn more about this later in the section on communication and suggestion.

I want to point out a few things about this approach. Look again at the first question:

"Would you like to do something that will give you a sense of how powerful your own mind can be?"

Notice this has the WIIFM in it, suggesting that the co-operator is going to find out how powerful their mind can be. How many people are going to say no to this? Who doesn't want to find out how powerful their mind can be? You'll probably get a yes about 99% of the time. By getting a yes at this point, you're starting to build what's called a 'yes set'. The idea behind a yes set is that if you get someone to reply 'yes' to several questions in a row, they are more likely to agree to your next suggestion or proposition.

The second part is:

"It's not really hypnosis, but it will give you a sense of how hypnosis works, yeah?"

At this point, you're taking away any pressure your co-operator might feel about either being hypnotised or experiencing hypnosis. You're saying it's *not* hypnosis but it will give them a sense of how hypnosis works. When you add the little tag question at the end ("...yeah?"), you're looking for nodding or other signs of an affirmative response that constitute the second 'yes' in your yes set. You are essentially asking your co-operator to affirm that they are willing to participate, but using command tonality on the tag question to nudge them towards an affirmative response (we'll cover this in more detail later).

Another layer you can usually add is that of leading their response to your tag question with a subtle nod of your own, again intended to evoke an affirmative response. Assuming this works well, you'll get three 'yes' responses, which is a pretty good yes set.

Note also that this piece of languaging delivers by *linguistic presupposition* the idea that hypnosis is a legitimate thing that does actually work. Such use of presupposition is a fundamental aspect of hypnotic suggestion work, which we we look at in more detail later.

Overall, I've fount the 'not hypnosis' frame to be a very useful in setting up for Hypnosis Without Trance. The co-operator isn't going to close their eyes and I'm not going to be saying 'sleep' or talk about them going 'deeper and deeper' or anything like that, so definitely 'not hypnosis' in the traditional sense. Instead, I'm offering an opportunity to engage in an intriguing experiment that will show them the power of their own mind, which most people love the idea of. It's a subtle but powerful frame.

We already briefly mentioned the idea of the WIIFM ("what's in it for me?") above. One way of leveraging this concept for buy-in is to run something along the following lines:

"Just imagine for a moment that hypnosis were simply about... connecting into yourself... into the deeper aspects of your mind... so as some very different, interesting and rewarding experiences can occur... if we could do a little bit of hypnosis today, and you could have a *really useful change happen in your life* as a result, what might that change be?"

What is implied (but not actually promised) here is that the person might stand a chance of achieving this useful and desirable change as a result of engaging. *And this might actually happen!* Remember the power of placebo? When we imply a possible outcome like this, we are tapping into that placebo potential. To make it a little more focused in this respect, whatever answer they gave we can weave it into the work.

Let's imagine they's answered, "I'd like to be more easy going". We'd simply squirrel that information away, start our facilitation (the next step in the five stage process) and at some appropriate point (usually when a phenomenon is manifesting - let's say a hand lifting all by itself) we would drop in a suggestion:

"...and as that hand continues to lift you can begin to wonder... when and where in your life... your inner mind... the creative intelligence within you... will surprise you with a more easy going response... perhaps just a more easy going way of being... and you might wonder whereabouts within yourself... you are already experiencing the most easy going... right now... because as that hand keeps rising... easily going upwards you can become more curious about what's possible."

As a general rule, make every hypnotic interaction a gift. Come from this place in your set up, and you will do much to encourage willing engagement.

This concludes our fundamentals on *set-up and pre-framing*. Developing a high level of craft in this area will take you a long way in your hypnotic endeavours. A good set-up leads to a good session just as surely as a poor set-up leads to a bad one.

Let's now move on to stage two.

Stage 2: Buy-in and Focus

This stage is about managing buy-in and establishing hypnotic focus. These two ideas are closely related. Regarding hypnotic focus, you will remember from the earlier section that hypnotic focus is an *uncritical* focus on current and anticipated experience. You want your co-operator to be 100% present in the moment - not an observer and especially not a *critical* observer.

We have already talked a lot about buy-in in our discussion of Stage 1. Stage 2 is primarily about developing responsiveness to our directions and suggestions without reservation or qualification. As such, our concern with buy-in at this stage is less about setting the frames that establish it and more about monitoring the *signs* that it is in place. For good results we need our co-operator to be in the moment, to follow our instructions precisely, and to move their attention and imagination in the ways that we direct. They will *only* do this if they've bought in to the ideas behind the process, the value in it for them, and to you as the facilitator. Conversely, if you are getting poor response to requests, directions and suggestions, it often indicates a lack of buy-in (though sometimes it indicates a more simple lack of understanding - either way, troubleshooting will be required). When you have the buy-in you need, you have the foundation for *hypnotic focus*.

Without buy-in, the session is unlikely to go well. If your co-operator has a critical, doubtful or sceptical attitude, this will scupper your chances of engendering hypnotic focus. Note that hypnotic focus isn't *just* about buy-in. You need the buy-in, which delivers the *uncritical* element of hypnotic focus, but you also need the actual focus itself.

I often put a private 'game frame' around this process of securing buy-in (that is, a private frame to shape my own thinking and engagement rather than that of the client). Looking at things through this frame, people go about their daily lives largely 'playing their own game'. They may not be aware of it, but they're playing their 'life game': running their everyday patterns of thought, movement and behaviour. They walk the way they walk, talk the way they talk and think the way they think.

When you work with them as a hypnotist, you need to stop them playing *their* game and get them to play *your* game instead. A lot of people are quite reluctant to do this which is why the the right framing is so important. Once you've got the general frame buy-in, you want your co-operator to buy in to the process itself, to get them doing what you want them to do and to follow your instructions.

As you go about securing and managing this buy-in, you will want to be looking out for what I call 'red flags' and 'green flags'. A green flag is any sign or bit of feedback from your co-operator that they are on board with the process and that the hypnotic loops you're establishing are manifesting. Green flags let you know you can proceed and perhaps escalate the session to a higher level if you want to. A red flag is anything that suggests your co-operator is trying to play *their* game rather than becoming absorbed in the process you are facilitating.

The more experienced you become, the more aptitude you will develop for spotting the 'micro-flags' on display in each moment (conveyed within the subtleties of expression and inflection). To begin with, however, it is useful to work with explicit 'flag tests'. These consist of questions, the answers to which will produce either green or red flags.

Flag test questions are almost always closed questions, meaning the answer has to be simply "yes" or "no". Generally speaking, our green flag response will be a "yes", but we don't just want any "yes", we want a completely *congruent* "yes". That is, a "yes" given without doubt or hesitation, supported by positive body language.

'Congruent', in this context, is a technical term borrowed from the therapy world meaning that what your co-operator says aligns with their inner view or experience. In the words of Carl Rogers, 'congruence' describes, "the match or fit between an individual's inner feelings and [their] outer display. The congruent person is genuine, real, integrated, whole, and transparent. The non-congruent person tries to impress, plays a role, puts up a front, and hides behind a facade." (https://www.nlpworld.co.uk/nlp-glossary/c/congruence)

In flag testing, whilst we are looking for clear and congruent 'yeses' to proceed, the *congruence* is more important than the yes itself. A congruent 'no' is entirely valid as it just means that the person doesn't wish to play, which is fine — there is no rule in the universe that says they must. What you need to be far more careful about are replies that *sound* quite positive but lack congruence and are therefore actually red flags.

For example, suppose you say, "Are you happy to use your imagination right now?" and your co-operator replies, "Yeah, I guess so." This is a *red* flag, *not* a green one. Although your co-operator is expressing a degree of agreement, it's only *partial* agreement and involves some hesitation. It's as if the prospective co-operator is saying, "Yeah, I will deign to do that", implying that they are still playing their own game and will only participate on their own terms. This isn't what you're looking for. 'Congruence' is all about the *quality* of the 'yes' you receive. Be clear: a 'yes' that indicates reserve, hesitation and a lack of commitment is a *red* flag, *not* a green one.

Here are some flag test questions that you may like to use, particularly in conjunction with the 'not hypnosis' frame that I gave you before.

"Do you have a good imagination?"

If your co-operator says 'no', this isn't necessarily a bad thing. They may sincerely believe they don't have a good imagination. It doesn't necessarily mean they're not playing our game. If you do get a "no" simply continue, "But you can imagine things? [command tonality!]".

This almost always elicits a 'yes' (unless your co-operator is trying to be difficult) because of course everyone *can* imagine things (even if they don't think they have a good imagination). Hence you're looking for a clear and emphatic 'yes' at this point. So, "Yeah, of course I can" (the subtext being "isn't that obvious?") is not the kind of 'yes' we're looking for. This is your co-operator saying "yes" from within their own game, which is, again, a red flag.

Let's assume, however, that you're getting green flag 'yes' responses at this stage. Your next question might be:

"Are you happy to use your imagination now?"

Again, it's a closed question and you want a clear, congruent green flag 'yes', indicating that your co-operator is open to co-operating as required. Once you get a clear, positive 'yes', you know you're pretty much good to go and can start making action requests for them to respond to. This is where we move to *building responsiveness*.

To build responsiveness (the traditional term 'compliance' is a legacy of old school, authoritarian thinking), you begin by giving your co-operator clear behavioural directions to respond to. The aim is to get them *used* to responding to you and to establish a *habit* of response. Every *clear* and *unhesitating* response you get at this stage is a green flag.

For example, you might say, "Could you put your feet flat on the ground?". You're looking for them to respond without hesitation or qualification, indicating that their critical faculty is now completely out of the picture. Your requests at this stage might be arbitrary (but always act like they are meaningful) or they may be functional in terms of what you might be setting up as a first loop. For example, if you intend to demonstrate a hand stick you might request, "Could you place your hand flat on the table?"

This combines a flag test with a functional set up request.

Sometimes, especially when you are starting out, it is useful to give a series of directions to both monitor quality of response and build the habit of responding:

> "Could you put your feet flat on the ground... [pause to allow response] and can I get you to take a really big breath in... [pause to allow response] and just let it out [monitoring response], just as you can allow your shoulders to relax [monitoring response]. And notice what it's like to just be here now and hear the sound of my voice."

This is *absolutely not* an 'output only' set of instructions; there is monitoring of response throughout. We're looking for our co-operator to respond fluidly to each request, breathing in and out when we ask them to.

Another useful method (especially in street hypnosis) is to reposition your co-operator in the working space. So, if they are standing up, you might direct them like this: "Could I just get you to stand over here?" An extra trick here, as you do this, is to use a light touch on the shoulders to guide them to where you want them to stand. The key is to pay attention to the tactile feedback you get: can you feel the your co-operator going *with* your movement (green flag)? Or are they subtly resisting (red flag)?

There are lots of little things like this you can do to build the responsiveness you need. They also serve as excellent flag tests so you know if the picture looks green or red.

To put this into the context of the game frame: when a prospective co-operator plays their own game, *they* choose their posture, where they sit or stand, how they orientate themselves in relation to other people and countless other details. By moving them out of their chosen posture and position, you're getting them out of their game. As a result they become much more open to direction, because they have been taken out of their habitual response sets. Physically moving them (gently guiding *not* pushing them around), altering their posture or sitting position, or intervening in their natural breathing patterns are all powerful ways to take them out of their everyday game and draw them into a new, hypnotic one.

Another tactic that relates to engendering buy-in and that fits in well at this stage is what's known as 'witch doctoring'. This is essentially a subtle framing device that is more about what you *do* than what you *say* (although that doing may use words). With witch doctoring, the idea is to use small touches of ritual and procedure to subtly suggest authority, purpose and meaning. For example, you might make a small adjustment to the position of someone's hand even if you don't really have a reason to do so. You do it purely to subtly *imply* you have a reason for doing it, which conveys expertise and therefore authority through the suggestion that you are going about things in a knowing and purposeful way.

To give an example, when I do my card stick sequence (a classic street hypnosis piece you can see me demo on YouTube) I put the card in the persons's hand, then lift the hand up and make some small positional adjustments. The likely assumption on their part is that I'm making these adjustments for a functional reason, which in turn *implies* something real must be going on. Also implied is that if I am attending to such subtleties, I must really know what I'm doing. In the co-operator's perception, this builds both my credibility as a facilitator as well as that of the process we are engaging in.

Another witch doctoring technique I use is to ask a question such as, "Are you left-handed or right-handed?" Even in cases where this doesn't matter, asking this question gives my co-operator the impression that I'm asking for a reason. Witch doctoring is a subtle yet powerful device for implying expertise and building plausibility, so do make good use of it!

So far, so good. You've got buy-in, you've asked questions, you've got some congruent 'yes' responses and green flags. You have given your co-operator directions and perhaps repositioned them a little. Your co-operator has responded fluidly, moved where you want them to move and taken a deep breath when you've asked them to (though you may not have had to do much work at all if you were getting good responses right off the bat). With all this accomplished, you can safely conclude they are buying in fully and that their critical faculty is currently offline.

This is the point where you move to establish hypnotic focus proper, by bringing your co-operator to the point where they are completely focused into *present* and *anticipated* experience. ('Anticipated' here means as directed by *you*, the hypnotist, *not* some random anticipation on the part of the co-operator that may or may not be useful.)

Your first task is to pull your co-operator fully into the present moment, fully experiencing what is happening *now*. One of the simplest ways to begin this is by setting up a point of visual focus for the purpose of limiting their eye movement. As you may be aware, people do a lot of 'thinking with their eyes'. You may have noticed that, when you ask someone a question, they usually move their eyes as they're accessing the answer. This movement is *not* arbitrary. It is part and parcel of the requisite processing for retrieving the answer. By limiting this you are, once again, shutting down their own game, this time by interfering with their default internal processing. In hypnotic facilitation, we do this simply by giving our co-operator a point of visual focus.

Let's look at the example of a hand stick facilitation to illustrate this. You set this up with the direction, "Ok, what I'd like for you to do is place your right hand flat on the table" (and you show them exactly how you want them to do this by modelling the movement with your own hand — more on this later). Getting a nice, fluid response to this (green flag) you go on to say, "With your hand flat on the table, I'd like you to just pick a point on that hand you can *focus on*... fully... and allow your focus to become fully absorbed in that point."

So you've coached your co-operator to choose a focal point and to fixate their eyes on it, thus taking them out of their own 'eye movement game'. However, this is only our entry point for hypnotic focus. Our next move is to bring them more fully into this present moment using our words, and we do this by *pacing* their current experience.

'Pacing', is a major concept in hypnotic communication. It essentially means reflecting back a person's current experience by verbal and non-verbal means. Non-verbal pacing might be undertaken by breathing in time with someone, or reacting to the same thing in the same way at the same time (joining them in their reaction, *not* mocking it). Here we are going to concern ourselves only with linguistic pacing, meaning using our words to reflect experience. For example, I could say that, right now, in *this* moment, you're reading this book... these words... and as you allow your eyes to move along each line, word by word, there's no need to pay attention to your breathing or the thoughts that you may be having as you continue to read.

You see how this works? I'm simply making accurate statements about your current experience. The fact that you are reading this book is beyond doubt. I also mentioned that you're breathing - but don't need to pay attention to this - and referred to thoughts that you may or may not be having. In doing all this, I am pacing your current experience. This gets you to focus on the current moment and pay attention to details of your current experience. This is what I mean by pacing.

It's worth mentioning here that pacing is always used to set up 'leading'. So in the reading example above, I started with pure pacing but then began to weave in leading suggestions: "There's no need to *pay attention* to your breathing" and so on. Pacing and leading is essentially the backbone of all hypnotic communication and, as such, we will be revisiting it again later.

When thinking about pacing, remember the concept of *visual*, *auditory* and *kinaesthetic* awareness. There are things that people *see*, things they *hear* and things they *feel*. (We're going to ignore smell and taste for the moment as they are not overly relevant unless you're doing hypnosis in a lavender field or a pig farm.) For example, suppose you're working with someone in a rather noisy pub and they are fixating on the back of their hand. You could say, "You can continue to look at the back of the hand... and as you see that hand now (visual pace), feeling the table underneath (kinaesthetic pace), you can notice the sounds around (auditory pace), taking you more deeply into the experience (lead)."

So here we are using our suggestion work to not only pace but also lead our co-operator more deeply into the experience of the moment. This is, of course, congruent with the aim of achieving hypnotic focus.

There's one final point I want to make about hypnotic focus. Don't just say the words and go through the motions: *always remain alert and aware.* Hypnosis is two people playing a game or, to return to the metaphor I used much earlier, dancing together. Always pay attention to the feedback you're receiving from your co-operator. If you're trying to pace and lead but your co-operator's eyes are wandering all over the place and they're fidgeting, you can assume they're *not* hypnotically focused. Pay attention to the red and green flags. A good green flag in this context is to see your co-operator maintaining steady, constant fixation on their chosen point. There are other good signs too, such as their breathing becoming more relaxed as they become more focused. The key is to always be monitoring to see that your co-operator is still paying attention and flowing along.

Something else to watch for here: while you're pacing, leading and building focus, there's no real need for your co-operator to say anything unless you ask a direct question. You may sometimes get people that want to respond verbally to everything. For example, you say, "As you continue to look at your hand...," and they say, "Uh huh" or something similar.

Should this happen, simply coach the engagement you want by saying something like, "As you continue to look at your hand... and let yourself become fully absorbed in this moment. *You don't have to say anything...* just allow yourself to have this experience... fully".

You're encouraging them not to say anything while drawing them more and more into the hypnotic focus.

So, that is hypnotic focus. Assuming you have achieved it, you are ready to move on to generating, testing and managing hypnotic loops. This is the phase where we start generating for our co-operator the kind of shifts in reality that we would classically call hypnotic phenomena.

Stage 3: Managing Hypnotic Loops

At this stage our focus becomes the shifting of our co-operator's experience of reality — the evocation of a 'hypnotic phenomenon'. We do this by guiding them into a new *hypnotic loop* appropriate for creating the desired result.

In actuality, we have already begun this process with our work at Stage 2, as establishing hypnotic focus is the first part of setting up our first loop. With hypnotic focus established, our next task is to transform the *content* of that hypnotic focus from the current perceived reality to a new, *created* one. We do this predominantly by the mechanism of pacing and leading - taking 'baby steps' from where we are to where we want to be. Each little shift redirecting attention and seeding new ideas through suggestion, we lead their cognitive processes in a creative act of phenomenological conjuring. This is where we leave Kansas behind!

First of all, you will want to have a very clear idea of where you want to take your co-operator and how. This is an important part of successful hypnosis *not* because you intend to get to your destination at all costs (you will likely need to be flexible in your facilitation, both with means and ends) but because it enables you to act *decisively* and with *certainty*. It is essential to convey an attitude of knowing exactly what you're doing and where you're going throughout the hypnosis session. If you don't do this, you will only sow doubt in your co-operator's mind.

To illustrate the process of establishing a hypnotic loop, let's continue to use the example of facilitating a hypnotic hand stick. As an aside: if you have never done this before, take a little time for yourself to imagine what it would be like to have your hand stuck to a table. Go full out with this: put your hand on a table and vividly imagine what it would be like if it were stuck and you couldn't lift it even if you really tried hard. Go as fully into the imagined experience as you can to the point you pretend with all that you are that it is really happening.

If you are really keen, be open to it *actually becoming real* for a time. It's always worth going through such exercises of imagination yourself before your first go at facilitating such an experience with someone else. It will really help to inform your communication and focus your intent.

OK, back to our facilitation. We will assume you have already engaged your co-operator's beliefs during the set-up stage by eliciting their position about hypnosis. You will also have plausibly framed this hypnosis session so that you have buy-in for both the process and for yourself as a credible operator. All of this would sit in the the *belief* box of the hypnotic loop (the four boxes, as you'll remember, being: Belief, Imagination, Physiology and Experience), although you're not doing much with this buy in at the moment because you're only at the stage of pacing experience for hypnotic focus.

At this point, your co-operator has their hand flat on the table (nice and solid as you modelled it for them when you made the request). They are looking at their hand, have a point of focus and are already absorbed in the moment due to your instruction and pacing. You pace their experience further, saying such things as, "And as you continue to look at your hand, you can feel your hand rested on the table... you can see the hand on the table... and you can feel the table underneath the hand". By pacing your co-operator's experience, here including what they can see and feel, you are working in the *experience* box of the hypnotic loop.

So you have been pacing and leading to build your co-operator's focus, and monitoring their response. Now you shift their focus into the actual experience of their hand being stuck. In doing this, we are working mainly in the *imagination* box of the loop, *pacing their experience* and leading through *description* and *suggestion*:

"As you continue to *see the hand* and *feel the hand pressing* on the table... you can almost begin to imagine how it would be to *experience now* a powerful glue *spreading*... between the hand and the table; just spreading completely between your hand and the table... soaking into the hand... and the hand *sinking in*... connecting in to the table itself... more and more fully... so as *that glue sets*... and the hand *sets in*... to the the table... *becoming solid* all the way through... as the hand locks and sticks in place... you can feel the rigidity...".

Here you have paced from what your co-operator can actually see, feel and experience to a description of glue spreading between the hand and the table. You have led them further into imagining what it would be like to feel that glue sticking and locking the hand in place. Note the language involved. Using a phrase like, "You can almost begin to imagine that...", mean there's really nothing for the co-operator to argue with. You're not giving a direct order such as, "Begin to imagine that..." As a general rule in hypnosis: always lead, never push. For most people, push on them and they will push back (it's a virtual cognitive reflex) which is why phrases like, "You can almost begin to imagine that..." work so well - nothing to push back on!

Notice how language works when you want to pace and lead. In particular, consider the use of metaphors. In this instance, we're using the metaphor of glue. You are not creating a reality in which glue is sticking your co-operator's hand to the table. You're creating a reality in which it is *as if* glue is sticking their hand to the table. When I do an arm lock, I often talk about it setting like plaster and becoming solid all the way through, or say it's becoming "solid like wood". Metaphors like this tap deeply into the human imagination.

When you choose metaphors for leading the imagination, please choose them wisely. It is apparently common (I've heard it more than too many times) for some hypnotists facilitating an 'eye lock' experience to use the metaphor "like superglue sticking your eyes shut". This is a poor choice because it would, of course, be deeply unpleasant and damaging if such a thing were to occur in real life. Using an unpleasant or frightening metaphor is not a great way to motivate a person to stay in your hypnosis game. They might well panic and jump out of that reality because they don't like it. When I facilitate an eye lock (it can have utility in changework), I will use a suggestion like "...to the point where you can... just for a time... begin to experience those eyes *comfortably stuck shut*..." Remember, we are using our language to shape experience, so consider carefully the *quality* of the experience that you want to shape. Take care to use metaphors and descriptions that don't involve worrying or alarming ideas and that might lead to negative reaction.

Let's return to our hand stick example. You have started generating the new reality by tapping into your co-operator's imagination, paying careful attention to their non-verbal responses as you go. You're continuing to monitor for green flags and indications that your co-operator is totally absorbed in the unfolding experience. These might be simply how their eyes are focused and the look on their face, but it might also be direct physiological responses to your suggestions, such as seeing their muscles tighten as you deliver suggestions for "locking". Red flags would be signs that the person is distracted, fidgeting, scratching their head with their other hand, looking at you with an expression of incredulity and so on.

It is useful to be able to create effects with multiple descriptions, especially ones that can overlap and support each other. Remember that some people respond to certain *ideodynamic* categories better than others. Also, keep in mind the concept of visual, auditory and kinaesthetic preferences. Occasionally, depending on the type of demonstration you're giving, you may also consider olfactory (smell) and gustatory (taste) descriptions. For example, you might invite a co-operator to imagine biting into a lemon to get their saliva flowing, or have someone bite into an onion while believing it's an apple. Just be aware of all the options you can explore when providing multiple descriptions. What your co-operator could see, hear, feel, smell and taste may all be important and useful in your descriptive work.

Back to our hand stick. By this point, you aim is to have your co-operator drawn into a new reality of 'lockedness' and 'stuckness' in the hand. Ideally, you are seeing lots of green flags that suggest they are fully along for the ride. If all this is so, it's time for a little test of this new reality, to get a clearer sense of how strongly it is manifesting. We will look at this test in a moment.

In the contrary situation where we are getting mostly red flags we are better off eliciting feedback with the question "...and what is it that is happening right now?" You *might* get a surprising answer like "my hand is stuck". If so, proceed! But whatever answer you get will contain useful feedback. For example, they may say "I'm just waiting to see if anything is going to happen". Here you might say "...and waiting to see [pacing their reality]... and waiting to see is one thing... and *becoming fully absorbed* quite something else. And I wonder... how might it be different for you if you were to *choose to let go of waiting*... and instead find out how *deeply into this experience you could go?*" I call this *coaching engagement* and it is something that few hypnotists do (I suspect because they are placing too much emphasis on their own role as operator and not enough on that of their co-operator). However, in our current scenario, we have mostly green flags, so we test.

Testing your progress is an important aspect of hypnotic facilitation as it is one of the surest ways to know whether you have successfully led your co-operator into the hypnotic loop. Positive results also strongly validate the experience for the co-operator, thus pulling them yet more fully into the loop. The tests you use can be classified as hard or soft.

Hard Tests

A hard test is one where there is no ambiguity around what's going to happen. It can be either digital or analogue.

A hard digital test is one that is either pass or fail. There is no in-between: it either works or it doesn't work. An example would be to say, "Go ahead, try and un*stick* your hand and find that you can't". The co-operator will find their hand is either stuck or it isn't. There's no in-between.

A hard analogue test is one that allows for some latitude or interpretation in terms of what constitutes 'success'. For example, during an arm levitation, you might say, "In a moment, when I touch you on the back of the hand, the hand will begin to lift up all by itself."

Here your co-operator's hand could rise quickly or slowly. The range of movement could be quite subtle or very dramatic. As long as there is *some* movement it can be deemed a success, even if it's not overly dramatic.

Soft Tests

A soft test involves asking your co-operator questions about the nature and quality of the experience they're having. For example: "And as you're noticing this now (pace), what's more stuck... your fingers or your palm? (lead)"

This soft test reinforces the loop you're asking about and also involves what's called a 'double bind'. A double bind works by providing only two options, both of which corroborate and reinforce the reality that you've lead your co-operator to create (a 'stuck' sensation in this instance).

Whichever side of the bind they choose, they are confirming the reality you have been hypnotically creating.

In this instance, whether they say 'fingers' or 'palm', they are affirming the presupposition of stuckness inherent within the suggestion. This gives you a very strong green flag on the soft test so you know you can proceed to a harder test should you wish to. It's often a good idea to go for soft tests before hard tests and analogue tests before digital ones.

Let's imagine you ask, "Which is more stuck, your fingers or your palm?" and your co-operator replies, "My fingers". You echo this reply as a pace: "Your fingers are more stuck." Then, you can lead with, "And as your fingers are *more stuck* and *sticking more now*... [touch their fingers to reinforce this] go ahead and *try* to lift one of those fingers, maybe even two of those fingers, and find that the *palm sticks even more*."

You have paced their reality and instantly led them into a stronger reinforcement of that reality. At the same time, you have introduced a harder challenge. You have asked them to try to lift their fingers while implying that it's going to be tough and difficult by stressing the word 'try'.

This is an important pattern:

- Listen to your co-operator's reply and echo it using their own language
- Pace the response
- Lead into a reinforcement of the loop
- Apply a stronger test, implying that they will find it stronger and more of a challenge

Having done all this, you should see that when your co-operator now tries to lift their fingers they are unable to do so. This shows us that physiology (box 3) is fully engaged in the loop. It's a change in their muscle response as a result of the the engagement of their *beliefs* (box 1) and the leading of their *imagination* (box 2).

Our co-operator tries to raise their fingers and finds they can't, because their *physiology* has shifted in accordance with *imagination*. They then *experience* their fingers being stuck which reinforces the *belief* in the process that's occurring: that they are somehow 'in hypnosis' and their fingers have become stuck as a result. At this point, we know the loop is well established and our co-operator is responding beautifully.

At this point, I would suggest that you observe your co-operator for a few seconds, checking to see that they are still focused and that they are struggling a little with this challenge of trying to raise their fingers. For example, you might see their muscles twitching a little as they experience this 'stuck' sensation.

As you observe them in this experience, it is useful to elicit what I call a *reality report*. This simply means asking a question in order to get a description of the co-operator's subjective reality. For example: "What's that like now as you *try* and un*stick* your finger and find that it just sticks more... and your palm sticks more?"

Beyond eliciting information that will be useful in generating further pacing suggestions, eliciting a reality report also serves to strengthen the loop by means of what Psychologist Robert Cialdini (in his book *Influence: The Psychology of Persuasion*) calls the consistency principle:

> *People like to be consistent with the things they have previously said or done.*

When our co-operator makes explicit statements about their experience they are, through the consistency principle, essentially committing themselves to that reality. Suppose the co-operator reports that it feels "really weird" or "strange". In making this statement they reinforce the reality for themselves and, in doing so, will feel further compelled to behave in ways that are *consistent* with it. By getting this verbal commitment we are making it far more likely that our co-operator will stay within the loop.

Another facet of eliciting reality reports is the acquisition of what I call *neurohandles*. A neurohandle is a word or a phrase taken from a co-operator's own description of their own experience, which therefore has a very specific meaning for them (in terms of that experience). If you ask your co-operator about what the hand stick feels like and they say, "Really weird", then 'really weird' is a neurohandle for them. Feeding this back to your co-operator can be a very powerful aspect of the hypnotic process.

If you respond using different terms, this is called a mismatch. For example:

"What's that like?"

"Really weird."

"Kind of strange, huh?"

Whilst we might consider 'kind of strange' and 'really weird' to mean essentially the same thing, they are likely to connect with the co-operator's reality in quite different ways. Whereas the original words will re-fire the experience that they came from, the alternative wording won't do so in the same way. In hypnotic facilitation we use words more to *evoke* than to *denote*... more like poetry than prose. Using the neurohandles of the co-operator allows you to tap into their neurology - their cognitive processes - more directly than you could otherwise. They almost literally become handles by which you can manoeuvre your co-operator into a stronger rendering of the loop or perhaps a different loop altogether.

When working with tests, I suggested you start with a very soft test and then escalate to a slightly harder test from which you elicit a reality report. Getting a favourable reality report, by which I mean anything that corroborates the loop and shows your co-operator's commitment to it, is a very clear green flag. It means you can escalate even further to a very strong digital test involving a significant challenge. Let's follow this sequence with our hand stick example:

"In fact, as your hand sticks even more now, go ahead and *try* and un*stick* it... find it sticks *even*

> *more fully, even more completely...* locking all the
> way through your wrist and your elbow and your
> shoulder [I'd be using light touches here implying
> the pathway of the spreading phenomenon] and
> your hand sticks. Go ahead try and un*stick* that
> hand... find it locks and sticks even more".

So here you're setting up a strong challenge, reinforcing
the reality for your co-operator of their hand being stuck
through the use of multiple descriptions. In this example,
I've suggested you refer to locking the wrist and elbow and
shoulder just to cover several options and increase the
chances of success (the 'belt and braces' approach).

Having issued this strong challenge, you will want to *see* a
behavioural response entirely congruent with the
suggested experience, such as being completely fixated
and clearly making an effort to unstick their hand, yet
finding they simply can't move it. You will get a range of
responses here, with the effect being more dramatic in
some cases than others. You might see your co-operator
really struggling and straining their muscles, as if they're
trying to lift a huge weight. Alternatively, you may just see
them staring, transfixed by a hand that's simply not
responding. Either scenario is a green flag, but may
differently inform your decisions as to where you go next.

If you do get a really strong response, you might choose to
escalate the challenge further still:

> "That's right, it just *sticks*. Go ahead, *really try*,
> you're a strong guy! Take hold of it with the other
> hand [show the action with your own hands] and
> *really try* [pantomime struggle to unstick], find it
> just *sticks more solidly*."

If you have reached this stage, you know that your co-operator is deeply in the loop: you escalated gently, tested gently, and now you can be very direct in terms of reinforcing and challenging the perceived reality that you have helped your co-operator to create.

To be clear, you do *not* want to push this hard until you have established, through progressive testing, that your co-operator is fully 'caught' in the hypnotic loop. However, when you do get this far, having tested your progress at each stage, you can push harder and harder. When you push hard and escalate the challenge to this point, it serves as a truly vivid demonstration for your co-operator that what they are engaging with has the power to change their reality. This is something that can be used to their benefit.

Let's recap. So far, you have:

- Seeded the idea of hypnosis.
- Elicited your co-operator's position on hypnosis.
- Framed for hypnosis and for plausibility regarding the types of phenomena you want to achieve.
- Set up hypnotic focus, achieved buy-in and performed flag tests.
- Paced and led the initial hypnotic focus into an altered reality.
- Tested this reality, progressing from soft tests to harder tests and then a strong challenge.

By this point, your co-operator's belief in the process (and its potential) will have greatly increased and deepened, and you can hook into this deepened belief in transitioning to another loop. This next loop may be intended to either further explore what's possible or to create shifts in experience for empowering or therapeutic purposes.

Loop Transitioning: Expansion and Transference

Having successfully established our first loop, we can now transition to a second loop if we wish to do so. In fact, we can go through as many loops as we choose, depending on how many altered realities we want to facilitate for our co-operator.

The simplest transitions involve *expansion* or *transference* of established hypnotic phenomena. With these transitions, we don't change the *type* of hypnotic phenomena our co-operator is experiencing. Instead, we change *where* it's experienced or the *extent* of the experience. For example, if you've already stuck someone's hand to the table, you might transfer that stuckness to another part of their body or expand the stuckness to cover a larger area of their body.

We can summarise the sequence for expansion as follows:

1. Clearly establish phenomena in one location.
2. Obtain a neurohandle for the *quality* of the experience in that location.
3. Facilitate the expansion of that quality to include additional areas.

Let's illustrate this sequence using the example of a *card stick*. This is a typical impromptu hypnosis opener for me, though it can work equally well in the office. Like the hand stick, this is an ideomotor effect. The co-operator is led into the experience of a business card being stuck between their fingers, to the point where they are unable to drop it (we will look in more detail at this elsewhere). We will have set this up by asking our co-operator to take hold of a business card (or coin, pen or other small object), gripped between thumb and index finger and held out in front of them so as they can visually focus on a point on the card. To establish the phenomenon, we will have moved through the initial stages of our 5 stage process to the point where their fingers are now physiologically locked and they are unable let go of the card. We have evoked a phenomenon of 'stuckness/lockedness' localised to the hand, which we now wish to extend to include the rest of the arm all the way up to the shoulder.

To set up for this expansion, we will want to first ensure that we have the phenomenon clearly and strongly in place, so we want to *challenge*. We also want to get a neurohandle we can use, so we want to go for some *reality reports* at the same time. Let's look at how this might unfold:

> Operator: "Go ahead, *try* and un*stick* that card, find it locks and *sticks even more solidly* as you *try* and un*stick it* ... really *try*. What happens when you *try* and un*stick* it and find it sticks more solidly? What's it like as it *sticks*... and you *try*?" [asking for a neurohandle for the *quality* at the end]
>
> Co-operator: *"I can't drop it."* [We get a reality report, but no neurohandle for the quality]
>
> Operator: "You *can't* drop it... and as you can't drop it... What's that hand like as you cant drop it?" [*Pacing* with the *reality report* then leading with a further question to get the neurohandle we want]
>
> Co-operator: *"Just completely rigid."*

So we get our *neurohandle* for the *quality* of the experience in the hand, which we will now use to broaden the area in which that quality is experienced.

Operator: "...completely rigid [feeding back the neurohandle]... and notice that completely rigid [lightly tapping the hand where the 'completely rigid' currently is] spreading all the way through the wrist, through the elbow, spreading all the way up into the shoulder now as you feel that [modelling the pathway as you go with further light taps]. Go ahead. Feel that completely rigid [neurohandle] all the way through your arm and into the shoulder *now*... What's that like with your whole arm *rigid now*?"

So we expand the stated quality using the neurohandle in conjunction with the non-verbal communication of touches. We started by associating the touch (a light, rhythmic tapping) with the neuro-handle: "...completely rigid [feeding back the neurohandle]... and notice that completely rigid [lightly tapping the hand where the 'completely rigid' currently is]..."

We close our suggestion set with a request for another reality report ("What's that like with your whole arm *rigid now*?") and, assuming we get a 'green flag' with the answer, we can move to a new challenge to validate. For example, you might say:

Operator: "Now with that rigid all the way through... and in the elbow... *try* and bend that elbow and find it just gets more rigid [whilst the operator simultaneously pantomimes appropriate struggle and rigidity]"

By this process we have successfully expanded the area affected by the hypnotic phenomenon and at the same time tested the effect.

The *transfer* transition is even more straightforward. Let's imagine you've got your co-operator's hand stuck to their head. You have asked for a reality report and tested that this phenomenon is securely established. You might give an instruction like this:

> "In a moment, I'm going to touch you on the back of the hand, and when I do that hand will become free... only as quickly *as you're feet stick solidly to the ground.* Your hand will become free when your *feet stick solidly* to the floor."

You touch your co-operator's hand. As soon as you do this, their hand becomes free and you encourage them to notice how their feet are "sticking more and more solidly to the floor as the hand becomes free". Through this simple sequence, you have transferred the phenomenon from your co-operator's hand to their foot.

You don't always have to transfer from stuckness in one place to stuckness somewhere else. There are other options. You can also transition into an entirely different category of hypnotic phenomena.

For example, suppose you have your hypnotee's hand stuck to their head. You can transfer into name amnesia by saying something like this:

> "In a moment I'm going to touch you on the back of the hand, and when I do, your hand will release from your head... but only as quickly as *your name disappears from your mind*, disappears so the harder you *try* to think about it, the further away it goes."

If you do this type of transfer, from one category of phenomena to another, don't just give the suggestion and wait to see if it works. Having shifted across, immediately strengthen and reinforce the new loop with your suggestion work. For example, you can give a suggestion like this:

> "In a moment when I touch on the back of the hand, your name will *disappear completely* from your mind, disappear completely, so the harder you *try* to think about it, the further away it just goes *now* [touch the hand]... Look at me. Look at me and *your name's gone now* as you look at me *and it's gone* and notice *nothing* where your name was. What happens as you try and say your name and there is *nothing* where it was? Nothing. Try and say it... and find there's *nothing*. Just *nothing*..." Just looking at me and trying to say it and there's *nothing*."

We are not simply *just* giving the suggestion, we are also reducing their scope for distracting thoughts by overloading them with suggestion and direction ("look at me"). Also, in this instance, the eye-contact works to inhibit their eye-accessing (which we talked about earlier) and to convey your own unflinching certainty in giving the suggestion. We are using a lot of languaging and sequencing, with pacing and leading, to draw them into the new loop, implanting thoughts and ideas in their head and leaving no room for their own thoughts.

You can follow this by gradually increasing the pauses between your words, which is a good way of soft testing the new loop. If you can allow your co-operator a little more processing space and you find they still remain in the loop, this is a big green flag. You can give more and more space and then go for a really hard test. Once you're sure you've got plenty of green flags for the amnesia, you can hard test it by saying something like:

> "Go ahead. Really *try* to remember, find it's just gone now, just disappeared. *Try* to remember it. Surely you can remember your own name? Try now. Look at me and try. Keep looking at me. Try to say your name."

Linking

In our example of *transferring*, we made use of a suggestion structure that *linked* from one phenomena to another via a defined moment or event (in our example, a touch on the back of the hand). We use this kind of linking a lot in managing the transition between loops, so it's well worth taking a closer look at.

There are two subtly different ways to handle linking: *pre-engineering* the link (which we used above) and *retro-engineering* the link. Before we look at both of these, please recognise that these methods are only to be used when the person you are working with has demonstrated themselves to be an excellent hypnotic responder. If they are not so good, you will likely need to continue with the richer, more real time facilitation based around pacing and leading. Let's look at the two types of linking.

The basic structure for pre-engineering goes like this: in a moment when I do X, you'll find that Y happens. For example, "In a moment when I touch you on the back of the hand, you'll find that your hand becomes free only as quickly as your feet stick deeply and solidly into the ground."

It's called *pre-engineering* because you're establishing what is *going* to happen and attaching it to a particular trigger, such as a touch on the back of the hand. When you 'pull' that trigger, you do the necessary work to complete the transfer to the new loop that you've pre-engineered. The strength of pre-engineering is that it allows you to 'front load' a lot of the details of the next loop, so it can come into being in it's entirety at the designated moment. Without creating this moment in time, the loop will have to be layered in the same way that the first loop was.

Retro-engineering works a little differently. Let's go back to the hand stick example. You could say something like, "And notice how your hand is now free," then touch the back of the hand and click your fingers. "Notice how the hand can become free now. You're just able to move it very easily." Then you ask:

"How was that?"

"*Weird.*"

"Do you know what's even weirder? As your hand released from the table *something very strange happened* [pause to build intrigue and anticipation]. As your hand became free, your coffee mug became *stuck to the table*. Go ahead and *very carefully* try and pick it up and find that it's *stuck solidly to the top of the table*."

Here we close one loop (the hand stick) but at the same time add a little curiosity hook by referring to 'something strange'. Then, having created this sense of intrigue, we deliver the suggestion and open the next loop. This is retro-engineering.

Both pre-engineering and retro-engineering can be used to link phenomena in the same category (such as ideomotor to ideomotor) or to transition to a different category (such as ideomotor to ideocognitive).

Nesting

The examples we've looked at so far have all been linear in nature (you close one loop and then open another), but you don't always have to use this approach. It's often more useful to leave one loop open and generate a new loop (or even several more) over the top of it. I refer to this as *nesting* hypnotic loops.

Here's an example of a sequence I might typically use. I start by generating stuckness in a specific area, move that stuckness around the co-operator's body, then leave their feet stuck to the floor. I then open a new loop for name amnesia *without* closing the stuck feet loop. I take them through this new loop, go for a hard challenge, then close the amnesia loop before asking, "And how are your feet?" because I never closed that loop. This is an example using two loops, but I could go three or even four deep. The only point to remember is that you can leave loop 1 open, establish loop 2, thoroughly explore loop 2 including some hard tests, close down loop 2 and then refer back to loop 1 before you close that loop as well.

I often use nesting as a structure for delivering empowering or therapeutic post-hypnotic suggestions. I open up a few loops and then put the suggestions directly in the middle, then close the loops back down. This tends to draw consciousness away from the suggestions, leaving them free from the clutches of the critical faculty.

Another advantage of nesting is that it allows us to really push the bounds of the work whilst providing a safety net. If we nest, we can go for progressively stronger phenomena until one breaks, at which point we have the conditions in place for a particular *no-fail manoeuvre* (from the HWT *No-fail Protocol*) called the *utility termination manoeuvre*.

To understand this, imagine we set up loop 1 as feet stuck to the floor. We leave it open and then successfully spin a name amnesia loop over the top. In turn, we leave this open and go for a negative hallucination (hypnotist becomes invisible to the hypnotee). We set this up with a pre-engineering linkage, fire it and test it and... it fails to take! Here's how we play this:

> Operator: "...go ahead open your eyes and find you see right through me..." [Operator steps to the side as soon as the co-operator's eyes open to see if they follow the movement or stay glazed and looking ahead. The co-operator follows the movement - a red flag]. "...and you can still see me..." [with this immediate and confident pace, the hypnotist retains 'ownership' of the facilitation.] "...and... how's that name? Try and say it?"

At this point one of two things will happen: either the name will still be gone or the name will have come back. If the name is still gone:

> Operator: "And the names still gone! That's curious!" [The operator will now simply act as if the negative hallucination attempt had never happened and get more reality reports confirming the strangeness of the name amnesia. This minimises the 'failure' and maximises the success.]

If, on the other hand, the name has come back:

Co-operator: "...Bob..."

Operator: "That's right because your name is yours..." ["That's right" implies that *this is what is supposed to be happening* and all of this is intended] "...and you find that you can now move your feet also... because they too are *your* feet."

The aim here is to behaviourally imply that this was the natural and intended end to the process. When I first started to use this manoeuvre I would make the framing explicit: "The best way to close hypnosis is to push the hypnotic reality so far out that normality snaps back in." I stopped doing this because it was unnecessary: the implicit suggestion carried by the *acting 'as if'* is much more powerful. Handled this way, the 'failure' is simply never framed as failure, and is therefore never perceived as such.

The Hypnotic Ladder

The final aspect of transitioning I want to mention is the concept of the *hypnotic ladder*. I've mentioned that people differ with regard to what they find plausible in terms of hypnotic phenomena. Nonetheless, there are certain phenomena that people *in general* seem to find more plausible than others. The idea of the hypnotic ladder is to *always progress from more plausible to less plausible.* For this reason, I generally tend to start off with ideomotor phenomena such as arm levitation or hand sticking because most people seem to consider such things as significantly more plausible than invisibility (not being able to see a person when they are standing right in front of them).

Following the principle of the hypnotic ladder, always start your demonstration with whatever hypnotic phenomenon you believe your co-operator will regard as most plausible. Once you have this phenomenon successfully established and tested to your satisfaction, you can progress to the second rung (something slightly less plausible) and the third rung (something even less plausible than that). For example: hand stick, then amnesia followed by positive hallucination (seeing something that isn't there) or negative (not seeing something that is there). This is a typical sequence I use for impromptu hypnosis demonstrations.

Generally speaking, don't rush ahead to the big, dramatic demonstrations. Proceed with a bit of caution and reduce the plausibility little by little, constantly testing your co-operator's commitment and belief on every 'rung' of the ladder. This increases the chances that the more outlandish phenomena will occur once you eventually get to them.

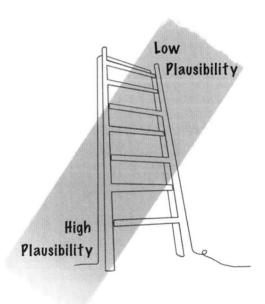

Stage 4: Loop Conclusion and Return of Control

Having taken our co-operator on a phenomenological tour of alternative realities, it's time to close the last loop and hand them back full 'control'. ('Control' is a problematic term but the easiest to work with for now.) Our aim is for them to continue their day free from any perceived 'hypnotic influence' (in case they're worried about this).

Under the old-school trance model, we would end the session by bringing them 'out' of hypnosis. Of course, within our model they were never in it, only engaging with a process. However, it's good to create a little ritual to mark the end of the process and send a clear signal to our co-operator that the hypnosis is over and things are 100% back to normal (maybe better than normal, but we'll get to that in Stage 5).

Perhaps the simplest way to do this is to ask your co-operator to take a deep breath and then exhale while you provide several suggestions regarding them returning to normal and being in control again. For this example, imagine the last loop you left open is your co-operator's feet being stuck to the floor and you wish to close this loop and end the session. You could start like this:

Operator: "So, how are those feet?"

Co-operator: "Well, they're still stuck to the ground."

Operator: "Still stuck? A strange thing, no? I tell you what, do me a favour, take a really, really big breath in [lead this with appropriate non-verbal gestures], that's right, and now breathe out... [still orchestrating non-verbally] just letting all of that go. Find those feet return to normal as everything returns to normal. You can move those feet now, can't you? It's easy. Everything returns to normal now. Now wasn't that a curious experience?"

So we invite our co-operator to demonstrate to themselves that everything has returned to normal, for example by moving their hand, feet or whatever was stuck. Then ask a question that involves the past tense:

"Wasn't that a strange experience?"

That's it. A short and easy ritual to end the hypnosis process. Even though there's not much to this 'ritual', you *do* need to include it as it represents a clear demarcation between hypnosis and normal reality. Your co-operator needs to be clear that they are back in the driving seat of their reality and hypnosis is now over. Back in my street hypnosis days, I would sometimes see people coming back at some of my fellow street hypnotists complaining that they felt they were still 'under' and being disturbed by this. This never happened to me, partly because I never played the frame that they were 'under' in the first place, but also because I was very clear in marking the close of the process *and* empowering them afterwards. All of which leads us neatly to the final stage.

Stage 5: Credit and Empowerment

This final stage is about ensuring your co-operator takes away something of value from their experience with you. You want them to be feeling good about everything that's happened and also to have set some conditions that may lead to it making a positive difference in their life.

When you get to this stage of the hypnosis session, your aim is to let your co-operator know that *they* created the experience using their inner mind and that they have the power within to create all manner of useful responses to whatever life might send their way. Make it clear that you didn't really do anything, only helped them to move their minds differently — *they* can take all the credit. This is a nice little gift to give them.

You can offer something like this:

> "You know, *you* created all this. And you might not have known, before now, that you have all these capabilities within you, but I'm wondering what difference it will make for you now... as you go forward in your life? Because, interestingly enough, this same deep, creative intelligence that has generated these experiences for you today is and will be always with you. And, the thing that is really interesting is, when you unlock it like this, some really cool things things tend to happen and you find yourself surprising yourself with new ways of being. New ways of responding. Spontaneously generating new creative solutions to the challenges that life sends your way. And this will show up for different people in different ways... so I'm really curious as to how this might show up for you!"

There is no fixed script for this. The general theme is: you have capabilities and a profound creative intelligence within you and what we have just done is to unlock these more fully. Now, what remains to be seen is how many cool ways this shows up for you in your life. You can riff around this with hypnotic language (which we will be learning about in the next chapter) in a variety of different ways, and I would advise scripting some different versions for yourself. The suggestion here is not that you memorise your scripts, but that you learn from the process of creating them.

In addition to making the session a gift for your co-operator, you are also strategically creating 'good karma' for yourself as you increase the likelihood that your co-operator will say positive things to others about you and their experience with you. This is useful for building your reputation, which feeds back into your credibility and authority, so aiding future buy-in. As you can see, this way of ending a session pays dividends for both you and your co-operator; much more so than trying to claim credit for yourself as some sort of 'mind control' expert.

The bottom line here is: always aim to make hypnosis as positive an experience as you can for your co-operator throughout the process and especially when you draw the session to a conclusion. Leave the people you work with feeling good, knowing they had a great time and that they have untapped power and capability within themselves.

3

Suggestion (1):

VERBAL PATTERNS

3. Suggestion (1): Verbal Patterns

This section and the next are both predominantly concerned with suggestion. To break this substantial topic down into slightly more manageable chunks, this chapter is mostly about *verbal* patterns while the next chapter, Chapter 4, is mostly about *nonverbal* patterns as well as what I refer to as 'magic words'. As you will see, the division between 'verbal' and 'nonverbal' is not a strict one and there is some degree of overlap between these chapters.

My aim in this chapter and the next is to share with you a range of communication tools you can use to take people through the hypnotic experience: pacing and leading them into the new hypnotic loops that will be shifting their perception of reality.

I don't intend to give a comprehensive academic overview of *all* possible linguistic permutations you can use in the facilitation of hypnosis (suggestion formulation is a very rich topic indeed if you wish to dive down that rabbit hole). Instead, I will focus on the most effective patterns you can use to successfully achieve the shifts in experience known as hypnotic phenomena. Of course, the material I've chosen to include is influenced by my own style and approach. Other teachers have different styles and use different patterns. I suggest you learn from as many hypnotists as possible, noting the communication principles they use and experimenting with them in your own work. I used to write hypnotic patterns from other hypnotists on flashcards, 'feeling in' to the language as I went.

Please don't just read this chapter and the next one passively, as you might read a newspaper or a novel. This material is here to be studied, practised and applied, rather than just simply read. Let the material sink in, go back over it, take notes, absorb it on a conscious level and then put it into practice.

One of the great things about the patterns and principles in these two chapters is that you can practise them even when you don't have a co-operator. You can learn and embed the patterns just by repeating them. When I was learning hypnotic language, I took a pattern I liked and repeated it over and over in my mind as I went about my daily business (using the flash cards I mentioned before). The next time I did any hypnosis, I made sure I used that particular pattern, played with it, tried a few variations and explored how and why it worked. I encourage you to do the same — not just learning these patterns but using them and having fun exploring how effective they can be.

So let's begin.

Pacing and Leading

We have already talked about pacing and leading in the last chapter, so I am not going to say too much more about it here. I want to start with it, however, simply to reiterate how important it is. It would be an overstatement to say that pacing and leading is the foundation for *all* hypnotic languaging, but only a *slight* overstatement!

From a Hypnosis Without Trance perspective, we do not 'put people into hypnosis' — we only move them from whichever reality (hypnotic loop) they are already in, into another. We move people from *where they are at to where we want them to be.* The basic mechanism for this transference is *pacing* and *leading*.

So, as you read these words... [pace] ...notice how you can read them a little slower... [lead] and as you read them a little slower... [pace] ...notice how you can become aware of your left foot... [lead] ...and really do... and as you become aware of that foot... [pace] ...and you slow your reading... [lead] ...notice the sensation on the sole of the foot... [lead] ...and as you notice the sensation... [pace] ...how would it be if that sensation became... just the tiniest bit more... numb..? [lead] ...and really notice that!

That was a simple pacing and leading structure that you will have engaged with more or less fully [pace], at least enough to see how it works [lead] by baby-stepping from *what is* to *what is becoming*... moment by moment.

Whatever else you are doing, always be pacing and leading.

Direction and Suggestion

The two fundamental forms of communication involved in hypnosis are *direction* and *suggestion*.

Directions are simple instructions meant intended to be *consciously* and *volitionally* followed by the co-operator. For example "close your eyes." In contrast, suggestions are crafted to elicit a response at the *unconscious* level. For example "...notice a tendency for those eyes to want to close..."

Effective hypnotic facilitation is built upon the skilful use of both directions and suggestions throughout the entire process. However, as a general rule, you mostly use directions when setting up the process: drawing your co-operator into hypnotic focus, setting up loops, using flag tests and building responsiveness and compliance. For example, you might say things like this:

"Could your put your feet flat on the ground?"

"Could you place your hand on the table?"

These are directions (albeit phrased as polite invitations) designed to elicit a volitional response. If your co-operator doesn't respond well to directions, it's highly unlikely that they will respond well to suggestions. Hence directions are how you test for buy-in and responsiveness. They are also useful in practical terms, such as when you need someone to sit in a particular place or perform a specific action.

There is nothing particularly artful about giving directions. Just make sure your directions are clear, unambiguous and easy for your co-operator to follow. The more clear and precise you are, the more likely it is that they will follow your directions as intended.

Some ways of giving directions are unquestionably more pleasant and therefore more efficacious than others. People tend to dislike having orders barked at them in the manner of a bad-tempered drill instructor. Essentially, your aim is here to be the clear leader of a collaboration, so it's best to express directions as *invitations*:

"*Can you* place your feet flat on the floor?"

"*Can you* take a big breath in and just let that out?"

In this context, 'Can you' is what's sometimes called a *conversational postulate*. In strictly grammatical terms, you're asking a question rather than issuing a direction.

However, your words will be *understood* as directions in the form of a polite request and people tend to respond accordingly. Another polite way to give a direction is to say something like:

> "What I would like *for you* to do is, I'd like *for you* to place your hand flat on the table."

This sounds gentler than just telling someone to do something so it's far less likely that you'll meet with any resistance. Note the wording *"for* you" rather than simply "you" (which you can think of as a subtle 'micro-WIIFM'!).

This is pretty much all that needs to be said about directions. For the rest of this section, we're going to focus on how to structure and give suggestions: communications that are crafted to elicit a response at an unconscious level.

Direct and Indirect Suggestion

To be fully rounded as a hypnotic communicator, you will want to be adept with both *direct* and *indirect* suggestions. Of the two, direct suggestion has the longer pedigree, coming from classic authoritarian hypnosis. A direct suggestion might sound like this:

"With every breath that you take, your eyes will stick more fully shut, locking more fully shut and now completely as you try to open them, they lock even more tightly closed."

You can see how direct this is. There is no ambiguity, just direct statements detailing precisely what's going to happen as if it were irrefutable fact. This is the essence of direct suggestion.

Indirect suggestion is a little more subtle and therefore tends to encounter less resistance. In fact, it gives people very little opportunity to resist even *if* they wanted to. Here's an example:

> "As you allow yourself to become aware of your breathing now, you may begin to notice a tendency for your eyelids to relax... and relaxing even more... and you may wonder how it would be for them to just relax so much so that they... just for a time... don't even work anymore.
>
> And, as you notice this... you can be aware that normally you can open your eyes whenever you wish... but maybe you'll want to know this different experience now... and if you do... you can *try* to open those eyes and find just how much they don't want to... as they're so comfortable and happy to remain relaxed and closed. You can *try* to battle them if you wish... or instead just enjoy the deep, pleasant relaxation... or maybe even enjoy both at the same time."

The outcome for both suggestion sets is approximately the same (eyes that won't open) but they are quite different in character and approach. The strength of the former is clarity, but this sword cuts both ways: what is simple and straightforward can be more easily outmanoeuvred by the co-operator's critical faculty if they feel so inclined. To some co-operators, direct suggestions can sound too straightforward and simplistic to really qualify as 'hypnosis', whereas others prefer the straightforward clarity. The indirect approach, on the other hand, is more subtle, offering fewer points of resistance as it *implies* more than it *states*. Due to its unusual nature, indirect suggestion can seem to many co-operators a better fit for their idea of 'communication with the unconscious mind'. To others, however, it may just seem unclear and vague. To get a better sense of the respective 'flavours', here are some more pairs of contrasting direct and indirect suggestions.

Direct: "When I click my fingers, your hand will begin to rise up from your lap."

Indirect: "A clicking of the fingers can sometimes free a hand to begin to rise... when you notice that it wants to... just lift."

Direct: "Your arm is becoming stiffer and stiffer, like a steel bar, becoming stiffer and stiffer, more and more rigid."

Indirect: "And as that arm floats there, you may notice a sense of solidity... growing... as it floats in that place... in that space. In fact as you feel that now... that arm... that sense... and you might wonder whether the wrist is slightly stiffer than the elbow... already... or if the elbow is slightly stiffer than the shoulder.... or the wrist... and what might be stiffening... the most rapidly."

Direct: "Look at me and find your name has gone from your mind."

Indirect: "What happens when you look at me and find your name has just disappeared... now... as if there's just nothing where it was... What's it like, to try and find a name when there is nothing where it was?"

These examples should convey the difference between the two approaches to suggestion. Notice that with indirect suggestions, the opportunities to push back are minimised as there is nothing directly stated to push back against. There's little for the critical faculty to get its teeth into. This is why indirect suggestions can be extremely useful. With direct suggestion, there is plenty of meat for the critical faculty to bite into so you absolutely must ensure you have a good level of buy-in for the suggestion to work.

Now we have created this dichotomy, it is time to dissolve it. Instead of thinking that all suggestions divide neatly into two clear groups, direct and indirect, think of all suggestion sets as lying somewhere on a range from very direct at one extreme to very indirect at the other. This gives you a lot of choice about how softly you want to introduce a particular suggestion or how hard you want to push it.

So, when should you lean more in a *direct* direction and when more in an *indirect* one? This is a good question. Some people, particularly in the NLP world, maintain that indirect suggestions are always superior to direct ones. This is not necessarily true. Every situation is different, presenting its own set of challenges and opportunities. As you do more and more hypnosis, you'll find yourself at different times in different places working in different contexts. In each case, you have to make a judgment about whether direct or indirect suggestions are going to be most effective. The more experience you develop, the more reliable your judgment will become.

Let me pass on what I can from my own experience. As a general rule, when I start a session I tend to give very clear directions but fairly *indirect* suggestions. This is because I know that if I push people too quickly they tend to push back. Once my co-operator is fully focused and in a loop, that's when I feel I can really start to push their reality using strong, direct suggestions.

I will close this discussion with a brief anecdote that says something about co-operator perceptions in this matter:

A friend of mine once went to see a hypnotist because he wanted to stop smoking. He left the session and lit up immediately, feeling most disgruntled about the whole experience. When I asked him about it he said: "The guy just told me to close my eyes and count backwards for a bit, then just told me that from now on I would no longer want to smoke and would be a non-smoker! What was that!? I'm not going to quit smoking just 'cause he's told me I'm going to."

Recognising this as a simple, old school, direct suggestion approach I asked my smoker friend what he had expected: "I don't know. I guess to have him tell me a weird story about a walrus riding down the street on a grand piano or something. And then to find that I mysteriously had no more interest in smoking". For my friend, the direct suggestion approach just lacked *plausibility* and so failed to get his 'buy-in'. But I have no doubt that at least some of that hypnotist's clients did buy-in and and did find it helped them in stopping smoking. The moral is, it pays to be flexible.

Positive and Negative Suggestions

There's a debate in the hypnosis world that I'd like to address here. It has to do with positive and negative suggestions. Some experts say that you should *always* use positive suggestions rather than negative ones. In other words, you should state what you *want* to happen rather than what you *don't* want to happen. Here's a quick example to clarify the difference:

Positive version: "You can go ahead, you can *try* to open your eyes, find they stick shut, stick completely shut."

Negative version: "You can go ahead, you can try to open your eyes and find you're unable to open them, you're unable to open your eyes."

In the positive version, you are saying, "find your eyes stick shut". You are stating exactly what you want to happen - "stick shut". In the negative version, saying "you will be unable to open them" is considered a negative suggestion because you're telling your co-operator that they will *not* be able to do something.

Those who advocate only using positive suggestions argue that the unconscious mind cannot process a negative. The classic example is: "Don't think of a pink elephant in ballet shoes". Of course, in order to follow the instruction you have to process it, which necessitates thinking of said pink elephant. This piece of chicanery is sometimes offered as evidence that the unconscious mind doesn't process negatives.

Now while there is something to this, the conclusion is a logical leap too far: to say that the concept has to be processed in order to be negated doesn't mean that that negation cannot happen. Although positive suggestions *may* be stronger than negative ones it is clear that the human mind is quite capable of processing both. That said, I do agree that agree that positive suggestions are still generally stronger for the reasons stated above: negative suggestions contain the seed of the action you do *not* want the person to perform ('open your eyes' in our example) and require an extra step in cognitive processing to negate what has been seeded.

Let me share here quick story of unintended hypnosis to illustrate how the careless use of negative suggestion can lead to unintended consequences.

When one of my daughters was very young and still potty training, there was one occasion when she was sat on a bean bag in our sitting room with no nappy (diaper) on, and my father-in-law came to visit. Upon seeing her, he said to her very directly, "Don't wee on the bean bag!" She paused for only a few seconds of thought before doing just that! Of course, the idea of 'weeing on the bean bag' had not entered her mischievous little mind until it was suggested.

While I agree that positive suggestions may generally be *stronger* than negative ones, this is not to say that you cannot use both during hypnosis. Suppose you say to your co-operator, "You will be unable to lift your hand." This is a negative suggestion. However, you can reinforce it with positive suggestions stating exactly what you want to see happen and what you want your co-operator to experience:

> "You will be unable to lift your hand [negative] as it sticks solidly to the table [positive]... sticking and locking solidly [positive]... so you *try* to lift the hand and find it sticks and locks [positive]." (Placing the emphasis on the 'try' and not on 'lift the hand'.)

Here's another example that combines a negative suggestion with several positive ones:

> "In a moment when I ask you to open your eyes, you will be unable to see me [negative]... you will look completely through me [positive], as if I'm not there, looking through me as if I'm completely invisible [positive]."

In both these examples, we've added positive suggestions to an initial negative one. Remember, our job is to shape experience and, in doing this, what we exclude is just as important as what we include (although once the exclusion is stated, we spend more focus on what *is* than what *is not*). Beyond this, there are other creative ways to use negative negations to seed ideas. One is the "you don't have to" pattern, which goes like this:

> "And as you continue to look at your hand... you don't have to notice your breathing or realise that with every moment that passes you're becoming more absorbed".

So here we are using a soft negative suggestion to pace (the breathing) and lead (becoming more absorbed). Notice how this works: even though you're saying, "you don't have to notice", you are in fact stating the effect or phenomenon that you would like your co-operator to notice! You are using a strong injunction ("don't") but wrapped in a 'softener' ("you don't have to..."), chosen to take pressure out of things while still leaving the suggested option open.

Here's another creative way to employ a negative:

> "As you continue feeling your hand on the table, I don't want you to find your hand sticking *yet*".

Here we are using the negative structure to imply that at some point the hand is going to be sticking, thus seeding the idea and building anticipation.

In conclusion, it certainly isn't true that negative suggestions don't work or that you should never use them, and indeed they can be artfully combined with positive suggestions in this craft of shaping experience. However, unless you are using negative wording in a strategic way (excluding as part of shaping, or using a soft negative to seed an idea), it is definitely best to lean towards positive suggestions as they more clearly evoke what is wanted.

Presupposition

Language operates on two levels: *explicit* and *implicit*. The explicit level of information is all that is directly stated within a sentence. The implicit level of information is everything that the sentence *presupposes* to be true but does not directly state.

Consider this example:

  "John climbed the mountain."

On the explicit level, this tells you about someone called John and something he did.

On the implicit level, it contains several presuppositions, the first being that someone called John exists. We don't necessarily know anything about John but the sentence clearly presupposes that he exists and that he can climb a mountain. The sentence also presupposes mountains exist and that people sometimes climb them, and that the mountain was climbable. (And this is by no means an exhaustive list of what is presupposed by the sentence.)

When we consider just how much is presupposed in our communications it becomes clear that, when someone talks to you in normal, everyday conversation, you cannot evaluate every single piece of information contained in every sentence. For this reason, if you ever want to question or debate a point within a sentence, you will tend to focus on the most obvious one. In this example, you might question whether it was true that John climbed the mountain. You wouldn't generally question whether John exists or if there's a mountain to be climbed. This tendency to question the most obvious point (if we're going to question anything at all) gives us, as hypnotists, a wonderful opportunity to slip ideas 'under the radar'.

In hypnotic facilitation, it is our aim for all our communications to evade the scrutiny of our co-operators *critical faculty* (old hypnosis parlance for the part of the mind that analyses what is being said and decides whether to accept or reject it). Obviously, we want our suggestions readily accepted and realised, so in delivering as much as possible by *presupposition*, we're far less likely to encounter analytical resistance.

To give an example, suppose we want to do an arm levitation. We've gone through the set-up, we've paced, led and engendered hypnotic focus and now we're beginning to set up the loop by establishing hypnotic focus. We have our co-operator focusing on a point on their hand and we are choosing our next suggestion. So, we could go direct and explicit here:

> "As you continue to focus on that point... and notice your breathing... the hand will begin to lift."

This might be OK if the co-operator has fully bought in to the process and their critical faculty has already taken a back seat. However, as we are early in the process and still establishing the first loop, it is safer to take things more slowly and to seed the ideas we want by presupposition:

"As you continue to focus on that point ... and you become aware of your breathing... you may begin to notice the hand... and its tendency to want to start lifting itself up... outside of consciousness... like it wants to pull up all by itself."

This wording here seeds the idea of the hand lifting by presupposing that a *tendency* for it to want to lift *exists*. The invitation to the critical faculty is to attend only to what is explicitly stated: whether the person is *noticing* the tendency for the hand to want to lift and *not* whether such a tendency exists. The 'facts' that the hand rising all by itself, outside of consciousness, is possible *and* that a tendency for it to happen exists is *all embedded by presupposition*.

You can use a number of specific structures to embed presuppositions within your suggestions. These are called *presuppositional generators* and most of them come from the NLP Milton Model (Richard Bandler and John Grinder's model of how pioneering hypnotherapist Milton Erickson used language in his work). As we take a look at these presuppositional generators, please notice how many of the examples are built around the *pacing and leading* structure. Also, be aware that there are many other hypnotic language principles at play in conjunction with those illustrated here. Truly effective hypnotic suggestions almost always result from the simultaneous interweaving of multiple principles.

Subordinate Clause of Time

One excellent presuppositional generator is the subordinate clause of time. Here we use terms such as 'before', 'after', 'during', 'as', 'since' etc. to create presupposition. For example:

> "Are you happy to experience hypnosis while your friends are watching?"

This structure serves to draw conscious attention towards 'while your friends are watching' and away from what is presupposed: that hypnosis exists, that happiness in experiencing it is possible and so forth. In presupposing these things we seed them as possibilities for what is to ensue.

Here's another example:

> "You will need to take a small number of slow clear breaths... while remaining focused... before you really start feeling your hand sticking now."

In this instance, we focus attention on the action we're asking our co-operator to perform (taking a small number of slow clear breaths).

The experience (the hand sticking) we are aiming to shape up is presupposed.

Here's a presuppositional structure that I often use that makes use of 'when':

> "What happens *when* you look at me and your name is gone now? As you look at me and it's gone."

This sequence draws attention to 'what happens when' whilst presupposing that the name has gone. Note that this particular example is in the form of a question. We'll be looking at other patterns involving questions later.

Another type of time-based presupposition involves *ordinal numerals* such as 'first', 'second', 'third' and so on:

> "As you are here... listening to the sound of my voice... you may begin to wonder which hand will be the *first* hand... to begin to lift all by itself."

Here the notion that the co-operator's hand will lift is presupposed. The only point offered for consideration is which hand will rise first.

Stated or Implied 'All'

The next type of presupposition involves the stated or implied use of the word 'all'. In the context of facilitating a hypnotic hand stick, it might sound like this:

> "I don't know what's more stuck: your fingers or your palm."

This presupposes that *all* parts of the co-operator's hand are stuck — the fingers *and* the palm. The only point they are invited to consider is *which* is *more* stuck. Here's another example:

> "As you feel that *stuck solid*... I don't know if you *feel that* all the way through into the shoulder or if it's just the elbow or the wrist that's *sticking more* and more *solidly now*... with each passing moment."

This invites the participant to assess the extent of the 'stuck' feeling:. Does the feeling extend all the way through the shoulder? Alternatively, does it seem to be confined to just the elbow and the wrist? The actual 'stuck' sensation itself is presupposed. This is one of my favourite presuppositional patterns.

Awareness Predicates

Another way to smuggle presuppositions into your work is to use awareness predicates such as 'know', 'aware', 'realise' and 'notice'. Here's an example:

> "And as you *notice* whereabouts that name is within your mind..."

What's presupposed here is that the co-operator's name has a *location* within their mind (once they buy in to this idea, we are able to change the location and thus the co-operator's experience of the name). The only point you're inviting the hypnotee to consider explicitly is whether they notice *where* in their mind it seems to be. That it *has* a location is implicit, suggested by presupposition only. After all, in order for you to either notice or not notice something, it has to be there to be noticed or not! Here's another example:

> "As you continue to look at the point up there on the wall, you can allow yourself to become *aware* of how deeply absorbed you're becoming now."

This example presupposes that the co-operator is becoming deeply absorbed. The only question is whether they're aware of it or not.

It's worth noting that awareness predicates are not only useful as a way to deliver suggestions via presupposition; they also serve the simpler function of clearly directing the co-operator's attention — which is a key aspect of managing hypnotic focus.

Adverbial Presuppositions

Next, we have presuppositions based on adverbs: words like 'deeply', 'easily' and 'wonderfully' that provide extra information about a verb. For example:

> "How easily can you relax as you place your hand on top of the table now?"

This example, built around 'easily', involves the presupposition that the hypnotee can relax as they place their hand on top of the table. As the conscious attention is drawn to how *easily* they can relax, what is given is that they can relax. (This example also contains an *embedded command* to place their hand on the table.) Another example:

> "And as you continue to see the hand in front of you... just allow yourself to feel *fully* that hand stuck in place."

Here, the adverb 'fully' covers the presupposition that the co-operator can feel, and also that the hand *is* stuck in place.

So that's adverbial presupposition... and I wonder how *extensively* you will find yourself making use of this in your own hypnotic work?

Temporal Presuppositions

You can also create presuppositions using words associated with the passing of time, such as 'begin', 'end', 'stop', 'start', 'continue', 'precede' and 'already'.

> "As you *continue* to notice your breathing, and as you *continue* to look at that point on your hand..."

The 'continue to notice' part presupposes that the co-operator is *already* noticing their breathing. Similarly, the second part, 'as you continue to look', presupposes that the co-operator is already looking at the point on their hand. Here's another example using the word 'begin':

> "You can *begin* to feel your hand sticking solidly to the table."

If we simply said, "you can feel..." the critical faulty could push back with, "no I can't". 'Begin' introduces an ambiguity: "has it begun yet or not?", presupposing that there is a feeling to begin involved. We are also presupposing that sticking is happening, as now it is time to begin to feel it.

Commentary Terms

The last group of presuppositional generators are commentary words. These are usually adverbs indicating a mood or emotion, such as 'fortunately', 'luckily', 'curiously' and 'happily'. For example:

> "*Weirdly* enough, as your hand was unsticking, your name just disappeared from your mind..."

This example starts with the commentary word 'weirdly', which immediately draws attention to the *quality* of the co-operator's experience. In doing this, the experience itself is presupposed. Only the matter of how the co-operator might feel about it (does it feel weird or not?) is offered up for discussion or assessment. Here's another example that you might say to someone who's got their hand flat on the table:

> "Now with your hand there, *obviously* you can feel the hand stuck flat out there on the table."

In this case, you have used the adverb 'obviously' to generate a suggestion sequence that 'paces and leads' through the blending of verifiable facts (the person's hand *is* 'there' and they can 'feel it') with 'suggestion by ambiguity'. 'Stuck flat out there on the table' is ostensibly a metaphorical use of the word 'stuck', but one that starts to seed the idea of 'stuckness', which is the experience we ultimately intend to elicit.

Another type of commentary presupposition involves the use of phrasing such as:

> "And as you continue to look at that card, I don't know if you can already notice *a really interesting thing* beginning to happen... probably still outside of consciousness.... though maybe you're already aware... of your feet beginning to stick deeply into the ground."

This commentary explicitly states that what is happening is 'really interesting'. *What* is claimed to be really interesting (the 'feet beginning to stick solidly') is entirely presupposed. This commentary method can be extremely useful when transitioning, delivering new suggestions or setting up a new loop (as in the last example). It can also be used in the form of a question, like this:

"Isn't that an interesting thing?"

or

"Isn't that curious?"

The great thing about this type of presupposition is that if you get agreement then you've also got the commitment and consistency principle working to deepen your co-operator's buy in.

I appreciate that generating presuppositions might, upon first encounter, seem quite technical and perhaps even a little complex. This is quite normal, and it is a feeling that all great hypnotists have experienced. I will say, however, that it is well worth mastering this work as presuppositions are really useful and powerful — not just for formal hypnosis, but also for everyday influencing. To start with, just be aware that we are all presupposing things all the time, whenever we speak to one another. As a learning exercise, you can take any piece of speech or written word and go presupposition hunting.

It will also pay dividends to go through each category and write out your own examples (just think of the experience you want to presuppose and get busy presupposing it). As with everything else taught in this book, you are better off playing with it than intellectualising over it. Start by simply appreciating how this aspect of language works, allow yourself to absorb it and then enjoy experimenting and creating with it.

Linkages

I've already discussed how important pacing and leading is in hypnotic facilitation. The essence of pacing and leading is to connect something that is happening to something you *want* to happen. Making this connection linguistically brings us neatly to the subject of *linkages* which, like presuppositional generators, comes from Richard Bandler and John Grinder's Milton Model.

We're going to look at three levels of linkage: weak, medium and strong. Note that these terms have nothing to do with power or effectiveness; weak linkages can often be more effective than strong ones because they are less likely to trigger the activity of our participant's critical faculty.

The weakest form of linkage is the 'and' linkage:

> "So you're breathing comfortably *and* hearing the sound of my voice *and* becoming curious about this pleasant experience of hypnosis."

This uses 'and' to link what is currently happening (the co-operator is breathing *and* hearing your voice) with what you want to happen (becoming curious about the experience of hypnosis). This wording also includes the presupposition that the co-operator is experiencing hypnosis in a pleasant way. Here's another example:

> "You can continue focusing on that point... *and* relaxing more fully... "

This uses 'and' to link 'focusing on that point' with 'relaxing more fully', the implication being that focusing on the point will deepen relaxation.

The medium strength of linkage involves the relationship between the timing of one event and another. It tends to feature words such as 'when', 'during', 'while' and 'as'. It could sound like this:

> "As you feel the weight of your body rest in the chair... you can continue to relax."

This links 'feeling the weight of your body' with 'continuing to relax'. Here's an example using 'while':

> "And while you try to bend that arm... you can find your feet begin to stick as well."

This links the co-operator's attempt to bend their locked arm with something else becoming stuck. This is one way to achieve a transition from the current loop to a new loop.

Finally, there's the strong causal linkage. This involves words pertaining to causality, such as 'makes', 'causes', 'forces', 'requires' 'creates' etc. Example:

> "Notice how every touch on the back of your hand makes your hand just that little bit more numb."

This statement implies strong causation. You're saying that the touch on the back of the hand is making the hand become more numb. Here's another example:

> "Try to bend your arm, *requiring* a strength there that locks it more solidly in place the more you try to bend it."

The use of 'requires' creates a strong link between the strength used and increased.

Those are the weak, medium and strong forms of linkage.

The general pattern is always the same: link what *is* happening to something you *want* to happen, which you'll recognise as the fundamental mechanism of pacing and leading. To re-emphasise: stronger is not necessary better as the stronger forms are often more likely to evoke challenge from the critical faculty, while the 'weaker' ones slip by without challenge.

In working to master these linkages, once again I suggest you begin by writing out patterns that make use of them. Once you've understood how these linkages work, I suggest you practise actually saying them out loud. You don't need anyone to practise on — you can pretend your couch cushion is your co-operator! The point is to get used to the flow and delivery of the languaging.

Just get the practise done!

Questions

In everyday life we mostly use questions to get answers. In hypnotic facilitation, however, we value them far more as a means to direct attention and seed ideas.

This first part, directing attention, works very simply. Suppose I ask:

> "What would it be like to just *relax* and *feel good*?
> Let go of everything and *just be* for a time?"

This wording directs the co-operator's attention to 'relaxing', 'feeling good', 'letting go' and 'just being'. In order for the co-operator to make sense of these ideas, they have to access them at least a little.

As hypnotic facilitators, we can then use our skills to blow on the embers of the ideas we have evoked, encouraging them to burst into flame.

The question form is also a good way to seed ideas through presupposition. When you ask someone a question, they will reflexively initiate a search within their mind for the answer. What's especially beautiful about this is that, as soon as this reflex kicks in, the person you're talking to will have *already* accepted the presuppositions embedded within the question (because they've already moved on from processing it to answering it)! It is this that makes question form such a powerful means to structure indirect suggestions during our facilitations.

There are two types of questions: open and closed. A closed question can only be answered yes or no. For example:

"Can you feel that locking now?"

This question simply and elegantly presupposes that locking is taking place, and in replying 'yes' or 'no', the co-operator implicitly accepts this to be so. The closed question delivers an indirect suggestion. The cooperator may, of course, do further processing that brings their critical faculty into play, but for the moment we have drawn them them at least a little further into the experience we are shaping.

This is true of all hypnotic work: it is never 'mind control', only influence towards a desired outcome. With every effective suggestion we stack the odds in favour of our intended outcome manifesting, but we can never attain absolute control, no matter how good we are. (If hypnosis really were mind control, your average stage hypnotist would be ruling the world rather than selling tickets to watch people cluck like chickens. This is not to denigrate the significant utility of hypnosis for the enrichment of people's lives.)

An open question is one that cannot simply be answered with 'yes' or 'no'. For example:

> "What is it like as you feel your hand sticking solidly to the table?"

Again, this presupposes the message you want to deliver to your co-operator's inner mind: that the hand is sticking solidly to the table. Open questions tend to elicit a *reality report* from the subject, yielding a *neurohandle* that you can make good use of in the ongoing facilitation.

The examples we've looked at so far are *leading* questions. They lead the co-operator's mind in a particular direction to strategically deliver a presuppositional payload. It is also sometimes useful to use a 'clean' (non-leading) question during hypnosis. For example, you could simply ask:

> "What's that like for you?"

This question doesn't lead the co-operator in any particular direction and is light on presupposition (it does presuppose that the experience is like *something* but avoids any suggestion as to what). We use this form for obtaining uncontaminated reality reports and it is of particular value when facilitating personal change (clinical hypnosis, hypnotherapy and hypnotic coaching).

The simple rule here is: use leading questions when you want to deliver suggestions by using presupposition and use clean questions when looking to get an uncontaminated reality report.

Another way to use question form that warrants special attention is in the generation of what I call the *Ouroboros pattern*. As you may know, the Ouroboros is the ancient symbol of a serpent eating its own tail (see below).

With this pattern we make use of the question reflex to ask a leading question that creates a strange, self-consuming mental loop (hence Ouroboros). Here's an example of using the pattern in a name amnesia facilitation:

> "What's that like when you look at me *and* your
> name's *gone now..?* like there's now nothing where
> it was... nothing! Notice nothing. Look at me...
> what's that like when you *try* to say that name and
> there's *nothing*?"

In this pattern, we are combining a few different elements that we have already looked at separately. We are exploiting the question reflex (the tendency people have to reflexively answer a question) to pull them into this self-referential loop. Our first question simply creates an association between looking at me (pace) and the name being gone (lead). The association is built using *and linkage* but delivered by the presupposition inherent in the question form. We then 'tailcoat' in an additional element: 'like there's nothing where it (the name) was'. Now we are ready to fire the Ouroboros pattern: what's that like when you *try* to say that name and there's *nothing*?

We are essentially asking them to say the name *only* when it is not there, but all of this is delivered by the presupposition in the 'what happens when' question. The whole thing starts chasing (or eating) itself, and all the time the mind of the co-operator stays chasing an answer to the question. What they are *not* doing is accessing their name. This is the Ouroboros pattern.

Some have stated, upon seeing me demonstrate this, that what I am evoking is confusion and not amnesia. This is a fair comment but, according to the principles of Hypnosis Without Trance, things become what they are believed to be (phenomenologically speaking). So when we evoke this confusion and successfully frame it as amnesia, this is exactly what it becomes in the experience of the co-operator.

Here's another element that involves tonality. It's possible to ask the same question but use different stress and intonation to change the meaning. Consider this example:

"What's that like, when your name's gone?!"

First, try asking this question out loud using the normal 'questioning' intonation, by which I mean your tone rises towards the end to suggest that you don't know the answer and are requesting information. Now try asking the same question but using a *command intonation*, by which I mean your voice goes down at the end as if you're telling your co-operator what is happening and stating a given fact. Using our tone in this way enables us to use questions as a Trojan Horse for statements and directions.

As a general rule, you will want to *avoid* using questioning intonation when using the question form to deliver suggestions as it makes you seem uncertain in your facilitation, so get into the habit of using the command intonation. There is an exception to this: when looking to use questioning tonality strategically to seed uncertainty. For example, sticking with the name amnesia facilitation [or 'demonstration'], when you have delivered the initial suggestions and seen them take you might ask:

"What was your name?"

In this case, you *would* use a questioning tone (along with pantomiming 'unable to remember' with your facial expressions) and avoid a *command* tone (you do *not* want them to answer).

Finally in this section, I want to mention tag questions: making a statement and then adding a little tag that turns it into a question inviting a positive response:

"So that feels weird, doesn't it?"

The little 'doesn't it' at the end, delivered in the right way, encourages a 'yes' response. Here's another example:

> "So that hand's fully stuck now, isn't it? So when
> you *try* and un*stick* it… it doesn't budge, does it?"

This involves two tag questions that encourage agreement.
To increase the effectiveness of the tag question, deliver it
with a look of 'commanding expectancy' on your face. This
makes it even more likely that you'll win the 'yes' response
you're looking for.

This concludes our overview of questions and how
powerful they can be. So how will you be putting questions
to good use in your own hypnotic work?

Anticipation Hooks

Whenever you evoke a sense of anticipation within your
co-operator, they will immediately become more receptive
to whatever it is they are anticipating; to whatever might
fill the 'void of anticipation', so to speak. One of the ways
we put this principle into practice in Hypnosis Without
Trance is by means of what I call *anticipation hooks*. Here's
an example. Imagine you're in the middle of a hand stick:

> "What happens when you try and un*stick* that
> hand?"

> "It's *totally stuck*."

> "It's totally stuck? That's interesting… totally stuck.
> Now here's the thing… (pause)."

When you say "here's the thing" and pause, the participant
(along with any onlookers) will start to wonder what you're
going to say next. You have created anticipation.

When people have this sense of anticipation, they want to know what you're going to add and so become highly receptive to whatever you're about to say or share with them. Here's another anticipation hook you might like:

> "You know, while you've been trying to un*stick* your hand, something *really* interesting has just happened... (pause)."

You pause just long enough to build the anticipation, to get your co-operator wondering about this 'interesting thing' and wanting to know what it could be. This can create the perfect conditions for a loop transition — we drop the anticipation hook, hang for a moment and then:

> "...your name has just disappeared from your mind, completely disappeared... gone now... (continue shaping the new loop)."

Remember that good hypnotic facilitation is *not* just about delivering suggestions. It is about a real-time, two-way interaction. This is relevant to making anticipation hooks work, because during the pause that follows the hook, you want to see that they are with you. Watch for the hint of anticipation in their facial expression that tells you they are hooked! Once you see this, you can deliver whatever content you want to put into that little pocket of anticipation. That said, if you can't see any such sign (sometimes it's quite subtle) it's better to assume the co-operator is hooked after a suitable beat than get caught in uncertainty. If in doubt, keep moving!

The anticipation hook is by no means an essential hypnotic facilitation tool but it *is* a very useful one. Play around with it and see what kind of results you can get.

Associative and Dissociative Language

When you're doing hypnosis and working to create a new reality for your co-operator, you want them to 'step away' from their old reality. Dissociative language is a way of encouraging this to happen.

Let's say we want to create an experience for your co-operators of their name being temporarily missing. It is fair to assume that they likely feel very intimately connected with their name. It *belongs* to them and they feel a strong *association* with it. What we want to do is to start creating a sense of distance from it, so we want to use more *dissociative* language when referring to it. For example:

> "And as I click my fingers, the name you had disappears completely. Look at me and try to say it. What was *the* name?"

Note how I say 'the name you had' rather than 'your name', using the past tense to presuppose the co-operator no longer has it. I also go on to refer to '*the* name' instead of '*your* name'. These choices are all dissociative in that they create distance between the participant and their name. This is the essence of dissociative language: replace possessive adjectives (my, your, their) with definite and indefinite articles (a, the)', and adjectives of proximity (this, these) with ones that create distance (that, those). To take another example, suppose your co-operator has their hand out in front of them. You could say:

> "As you look at *that* hand stuck out in front of you..."

You refer to 'that hand' rather than 'your hand'.

The strategic use of associative and dissociative language is particularly significant in hypnotic changework where we will often (but not always) want to create distance from the problem states and strong connection into resource states. If we're working with chronic pain, for example, we'd use dissociative language, combined with a reframing of experience e.g. 'those (dissociative) less than pleasant sensations' over 'your pain'. Conversely, if we're successful in helping the client to access a sense of comfort, we would want to refer to this (associative) comfort. This is a simple example, but as a rule of thumb: dissociate the client from problem states and experiences and associate them more fully into resource states and experiences.

In summary, dissociative language separates your co-operator from something they would ordinarily feel is part of them or belongs to them. This can help you to lead them away from the old reality (this thing is mine) to a new one (this thing can be seen in the abstract, nothing to do with me). Associative language takes someone into the experience you are looking to shape. We always use these two forms in strategic combination because, when a person dissociates from one position, they associate into another (wherever we go, here we are). Try this language pattern:

> "And what is it like when you try and unstick that hand (dissociative) inside of this (associative) experience of it sticking fully?"

Say that to yourself and notice what it evokes within you ('feel in' to it). Now repeat it with the 'this' and 'that' switched. How is it different for you? Are you already getting a sense of how this works now? Enjoy playing around with associative and dissociative language and seeing what kind of results you can get with it.

Playing with Time

When you're working to shift someone's reality, you can indirectly suggest that what may have been true in their *everyday reality* is no longer true in this *new reality* because something has changed. One way to do this is simply to change the tense you use. Consider the example of suggesting your co-operator has forgotten their name:

"Sorry, what *was* the name?"

Using the past tense implies that the name is no longer there (because otherwise you'd ask "What *is* your name?"). If you like, you can see this as another form of dissociation based on distance in time rather than space or location.

I use this in therapeutic contexts quite a lot. Let's say I've engaged my client hypnotically and we have created some difference in their experience of the problem. I've drawn them into a new hypnotic loop and their reality has shifted. Right now, in this new reality, they don't have the problem. Once I get an acknowledgement of this, I might say:

"And how's that *now*?"

By emphasising the word 'now', I am implying a contrast with an unspoken 'then', creating a subtle and indirect suggestion of change. As I deliver this type of suggestion, I monitor the client's verbal and non-verbal feedback to see how they are responding to it. In this instance, they may say something like, "Yes, I feel much freer," or look significantly more relaxed than when they were thinking about their problem before. I can then go on to say:

"Sorry, what *was* the problem that you *had*?"

By saying this, I'm strongly implying that whatever the problem may have been before, it clearly isn't a problem now. This wording also serves as a *challenge*, and is delivered with a questioning tonality and facial pantomime of 'struggling to remember'. The intention is to evoke an experience of amnesia for their problem (similar to the name amnesia examples we've previously discussed); the client's mind goes blank as they struggle to remember what the problem was.

This is a wonderful moment during hypnotherapy because it acts as such a strong 'convincer' that something has clearly changed. The client may have come to me with a problem they've had for a long time but now, in this moment, they not only don't have it but can't even remember what it was! Let me add that this is done very much with a sense of playfulness! It is unlikely you will have permanent amnesia happening so you are aiming only to leverage the moment for the sake of impact, *not* to get a lasting amnesia. Playing it in a fun way will achieve what is required.

Another way of playing with time is through the use of temporal prepositions such as 'before' and 'after':

"What are you noticing *now* that is different from *before*?"

"And *after* all this, what are you noticing that's different *now*?"

In many ways, implying difference with tense shifts, adverbs and prepositions is a whole craft in itself, but you can allow yourself to start exploring with it *now* with just these few simple ideas.

Amplifying Experience

Imagine you have just begun to draw someone into a new hypnotic reality - the loop is taking and their experience has already shifted but it isn't yet as rich as you want it to be. This is where it will serve to know how to intensify and increase that experience. A straightforward way to do this is to use comparative adjectives and phrases: 'bigger', 'more fully', 'heavier', 'lighter', 'harder' and so on. For example:

> "Notice how with each moment that passes... your hand is sticking *more* and *more fully*... becoming *more* and *more* stuck.. solidifying completely."

The best hypnosis provides a rich experience, so always look for opportunities to amplify and intensify in this way. Once you've led your co-operator into the loop, done your flag testing and got some green flags that they're beginning to manifest the desired phenomena, you can start to amplify the experience using this kind of language. The aim is to make the experience as powerful as possible, though *always* lead and *never* push.

One language pattern that's really great for amplification is the 'the more / the more' pattern:

> "*The more* you try to bend that arm, *the more* it just locks and sticks even more solidly now."

To be clear, this is a structure more than a language pattern, so you don't have to stick dogmatically to the precise words. You can vary it a little:

> "*The more* you try to bend that arm, *the stiffer* it becomes."

Here we are associating an *effort* with a *consequence* — specifically, that something intensifies or becomes even more difficult or puzzling. 'The more / the more' is very useful when you're looking to amplify experience.

As an aside, many problems that people bring into hypnotherapy also have a 'the more / the more' structure to them. This tends to occur when a person becomes too consciously preoccupied with trying to achieve something that is best left to unconscious processes. One example might be insomnia: the more the person *tries* to get to sleep, the more they interrupt the natural process of falling asleep. Sexual performance anxiety is another area where this can show up — the more the person worries about whether things will 'go well', the more likely it is that the things that need to work in that situation, won't.

For this reason, phenomena that are bound in place with 'the more / the more' patterns can serve as vivid and impactful metaphors for such problems. For example, you could set up a hand-stick, intensify it for a time with a 'the more / the more' pattern, and then shift into the suggestion: "Now, *stop* trying and find, as soon as you do... now... your hand becomes completely free [hand releases]... *now what was it you needed to let go of in order to create that freedom?*"

Returning to amplification, this is an important aspect of the craft to master, especially if you want to help people make changes in their lives. One simple and often effective approach to changework is to elicit resource states and hypnotically 'plug them in' to problem contexts. The aim here is not to replace the existing state with a new state, but to blow out the existing fixed pattern so as to create space for something new and better adapted to emerge.

When we do this, it is important that we get a resource state sufficiently powerful to do the job, and this is where skill with amplification comes in. Whether you are simply looking to play with hypnosis, or to create change, mastering this skill is a must.

Creating Associations in Abstract

At the beginning of this chapter we looked at *pacing and leading*, and saw how it works as a way of creating associations between something that is *already* happening (such as the co-operator fixating on a point) and something we *intend* to happen (such as their breathing starting to relax). However, this is *not* the only way to create and work with associations — remove the *pacing* element and we have what we call *association in abstract* (AIA). Consider this example:

> "Every time you *try* and un*stick* your hand, you'll find it becomes *more* and *more stuck*."

There is no pacing here. Instead, the wording very simply creates an association between the co-operator's efforts to unstick their hand and the hand becoming increasingly stuck. It is the lack of pacing here that designates it as 'in abstract' (pacing, in contrast, works with the concrete — what's actually happening). By way of contrast, a pacing version might sound like this:

> "As you *try* to un*stick* that hand now... *try* to unstick that hand... finding only that it *sticks more fully*."

In this case, we have the "as you..." working as a pacing device.

On the subject of amplifying experience, creating an AIA is another useful way to do this. Let's say you're working with someone whose arm is, through hypnotic facilitation, rigidly locked. You might amplify the experience by saying something like this:

> "Every time I touch your arm, notice how it becomes more *stiff*... more *rigid*... *even more solid* with every touch."

As you say this, you are making light touches to your co-operator's arm to fire off these created associations as you go, thus amplifying the rigidity within the arm.

Here's another example that involves making use of inevitable elements of the ongoing process:

> "With every word that I say, every thought that you think and every movement of your breath, your name will disappear... further over the horizon... leaving just a blank space where it was... just nothing... like a blank space..."

This associates the co-operator's name going further away with all the inevitable, ongoing activities that were mentioned: speaking, thinking and breathing. You know all these things are going to be happening so you use them as a vehicle to carry the name away.

AIA is the fundamental mechanism behind what's often called *post-hypnotic suggestion*. As the name suggests, a post-hypnotic suggestion is one intended to be triggered at some point subsequent to the hypnosis session. In theory, it could be triggered minutes, hours or days later, either once or on multiple occasions.

Here's an example that might be used in suggestion-based hypnotherapy:

> "From now on, every time someone offers you a cigarette you will say 'no', because you have now chosen health and freedom."

So the AIA is between being offered a cigarette and saying 'no', along with connection to those reasons for saying no (which would be specific and meaningful to that client, as you would have found their most powerful motivators).

Another example from 'classical' hypnosis might be how a hypnotist sets up an association between the word 'sleep' and the state of 'hypnotic trance' they have been led into:

> "From now on, you will find that every time I say the word 'sleep', you will return immediately to this pleasant and altered state..."

Technically, if this suggestion is sufficiently embedded, the hypnotist could meet their co-operator on another occasion, say "sleep" (usually with appropriate intention) and have the person drop immediately back into the associated state as a result. This concept tends to feature prominently in stage hypnosis skits. The stage hypnotists might say, "Every time you see me adjusting my tie you will dance like Michael Jackson," (or something equally hilarious and, no doubt, deserving of riotous applause).

Stage hypnosis, as you may have guessed, is really not my thing (sorry, stage hypnotists!) but I do use post-hypnotic suggestions in therapeutic contexts. For example, let's say I have a client who is responding well in facilitation. They have successfully shifted from the problem reality they were in before to a very resourceful reality. I can associate things in everyday life with this new resourceful reality, like this:

> "Each and every time you step through a doorway, you'll remember... at the deepest levels of who you are... that you have these new and profound capabilities within you."

So I set an association between opening or going through doorways, which is something the client is going to do many times a day, and connecting with these new, resourceful capabilities. This can be a useful device in therapeutic hypnosis and change work.

Creating associations is a fundamental aspect of the craft of hypnosis. Listen out for these associations when you see different hypnotists at work and think about the associations that would help *you* create the desired outcomes in your own work.

Pre-engineering Pattern

The pre-engineering pattern is a way of using AIA for setting up transitions into new loops. When setting up our first loop, we tend to need to progressively build the experience as we go. However, once the loop is built and our co-operator is responding strongly, we are able to set up the next loop with much more efficiency using pre-engineering. With pre-engineering we front-load many aspects required for the next loop onto a trigger, enabling us to fire them off all at once by 'pulling' that trigger. The pre-engineering pattern essentially consists of three elements:

1. Set-up: "In a moment but not yet, I'm going to x..."
2. Association: "When I do, y will happen..."
3. Consequence: "Only as quickly z..."

To illustrate this, let's imagine we have set up some sticking phenomena as a first loop. Our co-operator currently has their hand stuck to their head and is struggling to remove it. We know they are fully immersed in the new reality and highly responsive, so we can set up the next loop very simply using a pre-engineered transition. We decide we might transition into a *number block* for the next loop, so we want to unstick the hand in the current loop and open a new loop for the number 'four' disappearing from their mind. The three elements would sound something like this:

> "In a moment, but not yet, I'm going to touch you on the back of the hand [set-up] and when I do... your hand will *release fully* [association] only as quickly as the number between 'three' and 'five' disappears *absolutely* and *completely* from your mind just for a time and leaving a blank space... the *number gone* and *only* a *blank space* between 'three' and 'five' [consequence]... so you know when it goes blank *now,* [fire trigger by touching back of the hand]... and it's blank, and you *know* blank... and you can look at your hand... and go ahead and count those fingers and notice... blank... "

Let's look at how the three elements work together in this example.

> "In a moment but not yet..."

Here we set expectation ("In a moment...") but keep them where they are ("...but not yet").

This creates a container for us to fill with the details of the experience to come.

> "...I'm going to touch you on the back of the hand.
> When I do..."

This association element is where we establish what the trigger will be and, at the same time, what the effect on the *old* loop is going to be. The association pattern is: "I'm going to do *x* and when I do, *y* will happen." The next element is where we establish the specific *consequences* in terms of the new loop, by loading up the experiential content for that loop.

> "...only as quickly as the number between 'three'
> and 'five' disappears from your mind."

When all is set, we only need to pull the trigger to fire the transition to get them spinning into the new loop.

As a side note, the 'only as quickly' pattern doesn't always have to be part of a full transition. We can also use it to create a simple association between events in other contexts. For example, we might wish to set up an association between a hand continuing to lift and a growing sense of well-being:

> "And you can continue to experience that hand
> lifting up towards your face *only as quickly as* you
> begin to *feel good*... within yourself now...
> experiencing a growing sense of well-being..."

Rather than transitioning to a new loop we are using 'only as quickly' to draw new and useful elements into an existing loop.

In addition to handling straight transitions, we can also use the pre-engineering pattern to *nest* hypnotic loops. Nesting is the opening up a new loop while keeping the previous one running. When we use pre-engineering in nesting, we require only the first two elements. It would sound something like this:

"In a moment, but not yet [set-up], I'm going to click my fingers and when I do, the number between 'three' and 'five' will disappear completely from your mind and imagination [association]... just as surely as your hand *continues* to stick to your head [emphasising continuation of the existing loop]."

Overall, the pre-engineering pattern is a useful structure for creating a range of changes and effects, expanding effects or overlapping them. It is, however, not a magical incantation. If you haven't gone through the rest of the process I described in Chapter 3 (the set up, creating hypnotic focus, building response, soft testing then hard testing and so on), simply using this pattern on its own is unlikely to achieve much beyond getting you funny looks. Deploy this only when you *know* you have a responsive co-operator who is strongly manifesting the phenomena you have built through your initial work. At this point you can rock back from the more comprehensive facilitation work and start employing simpler and more direct suggestions such as those delivered through this pre-engineering structure.

Divide and Conquer Pattern

The divide and conquer pattern is a useful bit of business that I devised during my street hypnosis and mentalism days. Like the Ouroboros pattern, it works by creating a cognitive bind. To illustrate, let's use the example of a foot stick facilitation. We've reached the point where we have suggested that the feet will be stuck "deeply into the ground", and now we wish to go for a test:

> Operator: "Which is more stuck, the left foot or the right foot?"
>
> Co-operator: "Right foot."
>
> Operator: "Go ahead, *try* to un*stick* your right foot and find that the left foot *sticks even more solidly...*"

This reference to both the right and left foot divides the co-operator's focus and attention (hence the name of this pattern). Often, if you follow this up by asking, "Which is more stuck now?", the co-operator will tend to say it's the other foot.

This pattern works by setting up a strange kind of tension and confusion within your co-operator's mind that reinforces by *presupposition* the reality that you're suggesting to them. You can use the divide and conquer pattern with any phenomena that involves comparing two aspects of your co-operator's reality. For example:

> Operator: "Which is more stuck, your fingers or your palm?"
>
> Co-operator: "*My fingers.*"

Operator: "Notice that as your fingers are more
stuck now, you can go ahead you can try and
un*stick* one of those fingers, maybe even two of
those fingers, and find your palm sticks even more...
as you try and un*stick* those fingers now".

In this example, the word 'try' is used to imply that the
co-operator will experience difficulty in lifting their fingers.
We are also tying this effort to their palm sticking even
more, which divides their attention and gives rise to a
degree of confusion. ('Try' is one of the 'magic words', as I
call them, that we'll look at in the next chapter.)

Part of the utility of this pattern lies in it's inherent 'no-fail'
quality. To illustrate this, let's continue with the hand-stick
example and see how it might play out differently:

Operator: "...try and un*stick* one of those fingers,
maybe even two of those fingers, and find your
palm sticks even more... as you try and un*stick*
those fingers now"

Co-operator: [slowly lifts finger]

Operator: "That's right... and the finger lifts...
freeing itself now as the palm remains on the
table... and just continue to feel the table under the
palm... until it's time for the palm to lift too."

The original pattern makes no *explicit* claim that they will
be unable to lift the fingers. It merely implied it, so the
lifting of the finger doesn't actually negate anything that
has been stated (you have not been 'made wrong' by the
evidence of the action). This creates the opportunity to
continue the process by drawing the action into the work

and potentially set out in a fresh direction. As a rule of thumb, always bring anything that might take a co-operator out of the process, *into* the process first. Note that this pattern also involves an implicit *framing* action. By saying 'that's right' and bringing what's happened into the process, you have framed it as 'part of the process' rather than 'failure'. This whole response is what we call 'no-fail manoeuvring' within the HWT approach.

Some say the divide and conquer pattern may be helped by some basic facts of human anatomy. For example, with a palm flat on the table, lifting the fingers becomes harder due to the tendon stretch. Also, lifting the fingers causes the palm to become relatively more 'stuck'. There may also be a 'seesaw/teeter totter' effect for some — as they attempt to lift the fingers the palm presses down a little as a counter force. Similarly, with both feet on the ground, if a person takes a step with one foot they must necessarily shift their weight to the other, thus aligning with the stated reality of the other foot being 'more stuck'! Perhaps these anatomical details are factors in this pattern's effectiveness (working through the nexus of physiology is all part of working with the Hypnotic Loop model).

Personally speaking, I have got a lot of mileage out of this pattern in my more playful hypnotic facilitations, so I hope you get a lot from it it too.

The 'Feel That' Ambiguity

This pattern makes use of the HWT tactic of *retro-hijacking*. The basic idea is that we create fertile soil for *agreement* through the use of a specific *ambiguity*, into which we seed an *idea* that we wish to germinate.

To illustrate this we'll continue to use the example of a hand-stick to see how it might play in this context (I use this mostly with ideomotor phenomena and sometimes ideosensory such as anaesthesia or analgesia). Imagine you have your co-operators's hand on the table and you're aiming to generate an experience of 'stuckness'. You have them focusing on a point on the hand and have been hypnotically pacing current experience. Next, you start lightly and rhythmically tapping the back of the co-operators's hand (varying the spot, so you cover a large area of the hand). As you do this you say:

> "As you continue to look at the hand, you can feel
> that... [pause] that's right, feel that... [pause]
> starting to solidify... all the way through."

The question here is: does the phrase 'you can feel that' refer to the sensation of the tapping or the suggested solidification? This is what makes it an *ambiguity* (and a very useful ambiguity at that).

Here's how it works: As we touch the back of our co-operator's hand whilst simultaneously saying, "You can feel that...". Of course, they can only mentally agree with this statement as they will assume you are referring to the tapping. We pause for a beat, just enough to create the space needed for them to shift fully into an 'agreeing state' (this will be quick) which we then immediately load with our suggestion - "...starting to solidify." In receiving the idea whilst in an agreeing state, the path of least resistance for them is simply to continue with that state and thus find themselves agreeing with the suggestion by default.

To offer another example, let's say you wanted to set up analgesia in the hand in order to then transfer it to another part of the body where it might be needed (I've found this transfer approach is, for some reason, especially useful for toothache):

> "As you continue to look at the hand, you can feel that... [pause] that's right, feel that... [pause] starting to numb slightly... [get the numbness started then *amplify* as we have previously discussed]."

Same pattern, different application.

Here's one more example:

> "As you continue to look at the hand, you can feel that... [pause] that's right, feel that... [pause] deeper sense of profound possibility opening within you..."

And with that sense of profound possibility, I wonder how many applications *you* might find for this in your own work?

Suggestion (2):

Nonverbal Patterns

and Magic Words

4. Suggestion (2): Nonverbal Patterns and Magic Words

This chapter, like Chapter 3, is about patterns and techniques you can use to deliver effective suggestions in hypnotic facilitation. Whereas the preceding chapter focused on verbal patterns, in this chapter we are going to be focusing on nonverbal patterns along with a few extra-special 'magic words'.

Before we dive in, I want to repeat one point I made in the last chapter: please don't just *read* this material. Trying to appreciate these patterns just by reading about them is like trying to taste chocolate by reading its chemical formula. To get the full goodness from what we are exploring here you will need to not only reflect upon it deeply but also practise and experiment with it through applying it to your own hypnosis game. Words on a page can only convey so much - it is only by putting these patterns and techniques into practice that you can come to appreciate just how effective they can be.

My advice to you is this: get up, get out (or get on-line), find someone to practise your hypnosis with, use these patterns and *taste the chocolate*.

Power Beyond Words

When most people think about communication they tend to most immediately think in terms of words and language, but this is only a *part* of communication. Beyond words, we human beings communicate *so much* via intonation, posture, facial expression, gestures and many other subtle aspects of *nonverbal communication*, and almost all of this is processed entirely outside of consciousness. Let me emphasise this:

Almost all nonverbal communication is processed entirely outside of consciousness!

It is this fact that makes nonverbal communication so valuable to us as hypnotists.

When I say 'outside of consciousness' I really mean that it is beyond the clutches of the 'critical faculty'. Whereas a person can disagree with a statement or question a question, they cannot disagree with a gesture (or question it) if they are not consciously aware of it. This works in the other direction (output) too: as nonverbal communication is largely operating below the level of conscious awareness and therefore control (for those without training in its use), it tends to 'speak truth' by default.

Within the Ericksonian school, hypnosis is often regarded as a way to communicate with the 'unconscious mind'. If we take this to be a useful frame (and I think it often is), then working with nonverbal communication becomes hugely significant.

We are going to be looking at nonverbal communication from both an 'output' and 'input' perspective, as both the messages we send and the messages we receive are relevant to the game that we are playing. As a hypnotic facilitator, you're running a process that operates through feedback loops of communication between you and your co-operator (we've talked about this previously as a *hypnotic partnership*). To do so effectively, you need to be continually shifting, recalibrating and altering your approach and strategy based on the information you receive moment-by-moment from your co-operator. It is through this interplay that we dance our results out of the unfolding hypnotic process.

Clearly, the written word is not the ideal way to explore aspects of non-verbal communication. For this reason we will only really be scratching the surface here. If you would like to know more about nonverbal communication as it relates to hypnosis, I encourage you to engage with my online video resources (at HypnosisWithoutTrance.com).

Analogue Marking and Embedded Commands

Analogue marking is about *how* you say things rather than *what* you say. With analogue marking, your aim is to highlight certain elements within your suggestion work so as to mark them out for your co-operator's 'inner mind', thereby slipping under the radar of conscious awareness.

Throughout this book we have used the example of a hand stick to illustrate various principles, strategies and tactics. You may have noticed something about a particular application of italics that keeps cropping up:

"As you try and un*stick* that hand *more fully* now..."

Notice what you get when you eliminate everything that is *not* in italics:

"*Stick more fully.*"

Italics indicate the words that would, when spoken, be given extra stress or emphasis. I tend to think of this in terms of 'leaning on' the words I want to mark out a little more. In this instance when we take the 'leaned on' words on their own, they create what is called an 'embedded suggestion'. To appreciate this, say the words aloud right now, *leaning on* the words in italics to stress the embedded suggestion hidden within the broader sentence structure.

Using intonation is not the only way to highlight part of a suggestion or shape an embedded suggestion. You can also use *subtle* gestures. For example, you can raise your eyebrows as you say certain words, lift a finger in the air or gently touch your co-operator on the shoulder. These are all good ways to emphasise particular words in a way that the deeper aspects of the person's mind, outside of their consciousness, will notice.

Another way you might artfully mark out certain words is through the subtle use of eye movement. To use this method look predominantly at *one* of your co-operator's eyes and then, as you say the words you want to highlight, move your gaze to their other eye. You can do something similar on webcam by looking at the person on your screen as you speak, then shifting your gaze to the lens of the webcam to do the marking out.

To be clear, you don't always have to use analogue marking to highlight embedded suggestions as in the 'stick more fully now' example. To begin with, simply consider which words (and their corresponding ideas) you want to emphasise and, conversely, the ones that you want to play down. Let's look at the line "Go ahead, try and drop that and find that you cannot". Thinking about our outcome, if we were to emphasise thus:

> "Go ahead, try and *drop that* and find that you cannot."

We would be stressing the very thing we *don't* want to happen. This is not so good! Instead, we would want to stress it like this.

"Go ahead, *try* and drop that and find that you cannot"

Not only would we want to emphasise 'try' but we would also de-emphasise 'drop that' (which I do by speeding up on those words to 'skim over them').

Summing up, if there are words you want your co-operator to absorb at an unconscious level, you can mark them out using various methods such as intonation, subtle pauses, gestures and so on. You can also de-emphasise other elements by skimming over them quickly. I encourage you to explore with this idea, thinking about the words, ideas and messages you want the co-operator's inner mind to particularly notice and those you would prefer it to barely notice. Becoming adept at this aspect of hypnotic communication will significantly increase the impact of your hypnotic facilitation.

Pacing Nonverbal Messages

In previous chapters we looked at how we can pace a person's experience verbally. However, we have not yet discussed how we can also pace experience with *nonverbal* communication.

One basic way to do this is to match your overall 'rhythms' to theirs. So, if their breathing is quick and shallow, you make yours quick and shallow to pace, and then consider how you would like to lead towards a more relaxed breathing pattern (assuming this is your intention). When I do this I not only lead by changing my own breathing but also by making use of subtle and appropriate *orchestrating gestures*. Unfortunately, whilst these are very easy to demonstrate they are near impossible to describe, but I do want to flag that they are a part of the game.

In my live workshops, non-verbal pacing and leading is the first thing I teach before we use *any* words. I will dedicate at least a whole morning to this, progressing through a series of abstract exercises to develop the skill. Although I can't do the same in this book, here's one abstract 'drill' that you may get the opportunity to play with: if you find yourself walking with a friend *without* a pre-determined destination, notice who seems to be leading and who seems to be following. Aim to become the primary influencer by matching their pace and rhythm then leading with subtle course changes. I will not tell you how to take the lessons from this back into your hypnotic facilitation work. However, do this a few times and you will likely notice your attentional patterns changing during facilitation work and you will start to see more options for subtle influence.

To go into this a little further, I want to mention the concept of the *cognitive landscape* — an idea adapted from 'Clean Language and Symbolic Modelling' (the work of James Lawley and Penny Tompkins, following David Grove).

If you watch people describing their experience of, say, a recent event, you will notice that they naturally gesture with their hands. However, they do *not* simply gesture in a random fashion. They make gestures according to how, at an unconscious level, they are spatially organising their cognitive material. When people spatially organise in this way, they do so outside of consciousness. It follows that, when you work with this spatial organisation via your own gestures, you are operating purely at a level of unconscious influence.

The key point to appreciate is that gesturing is actually *part of* their cognition in that moment. Cognitive linguists George Lakoff and Mark Johnson (authors of 'Philosophy in the Flesh') have observed that spatial organisation is possibly the most fundamental aspect of our sense-making. People *move forward* in life or get *stuck*. They get *caught up* in problems and need to *get distance*. They may be *close* to someone emotionally or, alternatively, need *space* in the relationship. Lakoff and Johnson point out that these are not merely 'turns of phrase' but fundamental organisations in sense-making.

New Zealand hypnotist and therapist David Grove independently noticed that when his clients gestured during descriptions of their issues, they would gesture with consistency, often gesturing to particular spaces both within and relative to themselves. Grove found that by ensuring his own gesturing remained congruent with the spatial organisations the clients were demonstrating, he could be significantly more effective at facilitating generative changes within that client. This is essentially a sophisticated form of non-verbal pacing that I have found to be very powerful indeed when it comes to hypnotic facilitation, especially in the realm of changework.

Working with these these spatial organisations is largely a matter of being aware of where things the client mentions are cognitively 'placed', and then ensuring that you gesture to those same locations when you refer to them, much as if you were gesturing to items in the room. You may also change these cognitive locations - we'll look at an example of this shortly, with regard to facilitating the experience of name amnesia. Providing you do it well, this kind of work will be processed by your co-operator entirely at the unconscious level. Make no mistake, developing skill in this area is a game-changer when it comes to hypnotic facilitation and yet, incredibly, many traditional practitioners are almost entirely unaware that it even exists.

To illustrate working with *cognitive landscape*, let's look at the facilitation of name amnesia. We have already looked at some language patterns I might use in such a facilitation, but much of the work in my approach to this is done through working with spatial organisation. Assuming other aspects of the set-up have been taken care of, I begin by asking my co-operator whereabouts their name is in their mind or in their body (I support this with subtle gesture to the head and body). If they say in their mind, I ask:

"And whereabouts... [gesturing to head] in your mind? [command tonality]"

What will usually happen here is that they will gesture to a location and support that gesture with some words like "right here". My aim is to get them to gesture to the specific location, so if they just said "in the middle" I'd say "whereabouts in the middle" and subtly move my head as if trying to see it (this communication *never* gets spotted consciously but is almost always responded to).

As I do all this, I am monitoring the nonverbal *feedback* the whole time, looking for fluid responses and engagement.

In the same way that I look for a clear and congruent 'yes' during flag tests, in this case I am looking for a clear and congruent gesture. So, if they gesture vaguely towards their head and say, "I don't know, probably up there somewhere," whilst subtly shaking their head, I'd take that as a sign that they are not really buying-in or engaging. On the other hand, if they were to fluidly gesture towards a specific location (especially if accompanied by congruent eye movement), I know I have buy-in and some solid spatial organisation to work with. From here I pace this by gesturing towards the location of the name as well as using any relevant *neurohandles* they may have offered. Once paced, I can lead either by subtle gesture (which I use in conversational hypnosis a lot) or by explicitly *pantomiming* taking the name and moving it to a different location.

I don't suggest you use 'mirroring' at this point. Do *not* gesture to the equivalent point on your own head because this isn't within your co-operator's cognitive landscape. They may be able to map from your head to theirs but this would pull them away from the appropriate hypnotic focus as their attention gets drawn into the work of translation.

To look at this in the context of hypnotic changework, a client might say something like, "I just can't get past this block," while gesturing to a space in front of them. If you were to *mirror* this gesture, you would gesture to an equivalent space in front of *yourself* when referring to the client's 'block'. However, you will connect far more powerfully by gesturing towards the same space that they gestured towards. Work with the organisation as presented and all will go smoothly.

I make this point because the method of casually 'mirroring' another person's gestures is often taught by NLP-influenced communication trainers as a way to build rapport. This is absolutely fine if building rapport is your main concern but this is *not* what we are doing here: this is psychoactive facilitation *not* rapport-building. As David Grove put it, our aim is not so much to gain interpersonal rapport as to put someone more fully in rapport with their own experience.

Moving on from spatial organisation, another way of pacing non-verbal information from your hypnotee is to use small words and notes of encouragement such as, "That's right" or "That's it". So as you're facilitating the process of drawing them into a loop, you're monitoring for desired quality of response and 'green flags' — any actions or responses that are congruent with whatever you want to create. When you see such responses you want to encourage them. For example, you may see your co-operator soften their breathing a little in response to a suggestion of 'letting go', so you acknowledge and validate this with a, "That's right". To be clear, your co-operator might not even be consciously aware of what they did (shifting breathing) but by commenting on it in an encouraging way, you validate the accompanying state and overall direction of travel for the process. You are still pacing their actions and providing encouragement on a subconscious level.

Of course, you can highlight it more explicitly as well: when your co-operator takes a deep breath, you might say, "That's right, just breathe in now as you continue to look at that point." By saying this, you pace the nonverbal action and make it more explicitly a part of the hypnotic loop.

As a general rule, whenever you notice signs of *hypnotic focus* or the manifestation of desired phenomenon, encourage what you are seeing with something like, "That's it, continuing to become fully absorbed," or, "There you go... notice that...". Essentially, anything that highlights the nonverbal happening will suffice.

There's one last point I'd like to make about pacing nonverbal behaviour. If you have instructed your co-operator to fixate on a particular focal point, it's a good idea for you to direct *your* eyes towards that point as well. Make your focus of attention the same as theirs (or at least as far as it's practical to do so). I call this *taking a shared perspective*. When I'm doing my card stick, I stand *next to* my co-operator so I can focus my attention exactly where I wish them to focus theirs (share their perspective) and so better join them in the reality we are shaping.

Another major benefit of taking a shared perspective in 'eyes open' work is that it will keep you and your co-operator out of 'social eye-contact'. This is essential as such eye-contact risks pulling the co-operator out of the hypnotic experience you are facilitating by pulling them into their innate 'social game'. This is entirely contrary to what we want. People reflexively respond to eye contact, so be careful not to draw it during hypnotic facilitation unless you intend to use it strategically.

As a general rule, I suggest you keep people focused on where the action is. Nonverbal communication is key to doing this. Assuming you have successfully established yourself as the leader of the dynamic, your co-operator's focus and attention will be hugely influenced by your own throughout the process. Knowing this, and knowing how to make use of it, will pay significant dividends in all your facilitation work.

If you want to find out more about symbolic modelling and Clean Language, which is a rich subject in itself, search online for David Grove, James Lawley and Penny Tompkins. I also teach Grovian approaches as part of my Online Deep Apprenticeship (details at HypnosisWithoutTrance.com).

Shared Lucid Dreaming

Considering all that we have discussed in the preceding section, I want to suggest an idea that you may well find makes all of this considerably easier: instead of facilitating hypnosis from a purely technical perspective, as much as you can, start fully entering the experiences *along with* your co-operator.

To borrow the words of my friend and fellow hypnotist Michael Perez: "When I'm doing hypnosis it's like I'm lucid dreaming and the client is included."

I sometimes flip this round (especially when I'm facilitating in a changework context): it's like my client is lucid dreaming and I'm included.

Whichever way, the notion of the *shared lucid dream* is really useful. By 'entering the dream' with the client, it becomes easier to interact consistently and congruently with the organisation and 'logic' of the dream. The more fully absorbed you are, the more effortlessly your words and gestures will match what is happening; the more closely they match, the more fully your co-operator will be drawn in.

This way of working can be more challenging when you're starting out because there *are* technical elements to be learned and integrated. However, once you have those elements largely in place, the whole process of effective and artful facilitation is better served by a shift into this different realm. If you are starting out, just be aware that this is a possibility. If you are experienced, notice to what extent you already operate like this, and how much more fully you could!

Pantomiming

Pantomiming in this context refers to the use of nonverbal communication to enhance your suggestions and directions. Essentially, when you communicate with your co-operator, you ensure that you always communicate not just with your words but with your entire body, being and presence. Sometimes this might be subtle and sometimes very clear, but it should always be there in what you do.

Let's suppose we set up for hypnosis and have decided to move in the direction of a hand stick. We wish to have our co-operator place their hand on the table, but we want it placed firmly on the table and not just lightly resting (we want to set congruent conditions for locking right from the get go). Instead of just asking them with words alone, we also *pantomime* the action for them by placing our own hand down with the requisite firmness and locking our own muscles tightly in place to show them exactly what to do. This way we suggest our intention nonverbally even *before* we state it explicitly. In short, if you want them to place their hand solidly and flatly on the table, perform the action and show them what you want to see, concurrent with the linguistic direction, "I'd like you to place your hand flat on the table". This type of suggestion is very powerful indeed.

To be clear: do *not* explicitly draw attention to this pantomiming, just let it be part of the ongoing flow of communication. You would never say, "Do it like this," or, "Watch me" or anything like that. You want the pantomiming to be in 'hidden in plain sight' as part of the flow of the action.

Here's another example. Imagine you have someone with their hand stuck to their head and you want them to try to remove it, suggesting that they'll find this difficult and a struggle. When you give this suggestion, *pantomime it yourself*, demonstrating the kind of struggle you expect them to display as you give the suggestion. This talks directly to the deeper part of your co-operators's mind that is creating the altered reality and that is switched on to this kind of nonverbal communication. This is sometimes called *analogue communication* because your actions and everything you show to your co-operator is directly analogous to the message you want to convey.

When you communicate with your entire body, it often lends a deeper, richer meaning to your vocal tone by default. Going back to the hand-stuck-on-head example, when you pantomime the struggle of removing your hand, it's hard to do that without putting the struggle into your voice as well, so you end up with a fully congruent 'dual-channel' communication.

It's worth mentioning here that I pantomime my suggestions even when my co-operator's eyes are closed and they cannot see me *because* what I'm pantomiming is still partly conveyed in my vocal tone. This is easy to do during a shared lucid dream because the pantomiming is never contrived, only a natural part of the dream manifesting as real.

Another aspect of pantomiming that I make extensive use of in phenomena work is the use of small, dramatic flourishes to specific moments in the process. For example, if I'm going to release someone's stuck hand, I will add a small flourish or marker such as a click of the fingers, or perform a 'release' gesture of loose finger movements, whilst moving my hand back and away (again, far easier to demonstrate than it is to describe).

Having mentioned finger clicks, let me add here that you can often use them to emphasise particular moments or events. For instance, if you want to amplify an experience of sticking, you can click your fingers while you say something like, "Feel that hand now *sticking* more solidly, *more* rigidly, *more* completely to the table...", synchronising the clicks with the words/syllables in italics. Clicking your fingers marks those words with something that culturally signifies action and rapid change. You often see magicians clicking their fingers to highlight a magical moment. As hypnotists, we want to do the same, to create magical shifts in reality.

There's another point I want to make about the vocal tone you use to deliver indirect suggestions. In the section on 'Implying difference with tense', I mentioned shifting to the past tense to dissociate your co-operator from their normal reality:

"Sorry, what *was* the name? It *was*..? what *was*..?"

As you say something like this, you can enhance it significantly by using your facial expression and tone of voice to convey a sense of confusion. You are pantomiming the very sense of confusion you are aiming to evoke.

This technique of suggestion-via-pantomiming is also highly effective in change work. Imagine you have taken your client through a series of hypnotic manoeuvres for the purpose of achieving change. You've reached the point where they can no longer access the negative emotions that were previously associated with the problem. At this point, you can say something like:

"I'm sorry, what was it, what was the problem?"

You say this in an almost 'tongue-in-cheek' way, seeding the idea of forgetfulness (or an inability to access the 'problem') and evoking the sense of it via your vocal tone and facial expression.

I also use pantomiming during what I call 'curiosity framing'. Curiosity is a powerful state because it engenders engagement, so you often want to evoke curiosity in people you work with. The easiest way to do this is to pantomime your *own* sense of curiosity, via your facial expression and vocal tone. You can occasionally add to the effect by saying something explicit like, "Isn't that a curious thing?", but the bulk of the work is done through pantomime (such as touching your chin in the 'philosopher's pose' along with a quizzical look) and voice tone.

The overall message here is: always use the expressiveness of your voice, face and body to convey tone and emotion, because they are powerful tools of suggestion and influence. Indeed, in so many ways, they are *much* more powerful than the actual words you say.

Magic Words

In completing this tour of hypnotic communication I want to return once again to hypnotic language, taking a look in particular at some words that are especially useful to us as hypnotists.

Please note, in order to keep things concise this is not intended as an exhaustive list of these hypnotic 'magic 'words, only my 'pick of the best'. You may have or find other words that you would choose to include on your version of this list that are missing from mine.

Try

'Try' is a hugely important word when you're testing your work through issuing challenges because it implies the notion of difficulty (or even outright) failure rather than ease. If I said, "I recently tried to run a marathon", you would immediately know that I didn't succeed because the verb 'try' implies failure when referring to a past event. In a similar way, if I use 'try' with reference to a future event, such as, "I'm going to try to run a marathon next month", you would sense that I'm not particularly confident of succeeding.

The fact that 'try' carries these connotations of difficulty and/or failure makes it very useful in hypnosis for *suggesting* such things. Look at these typical hypnotic directions:

> "*Try* to stand and find that your legs just won't move... go ahead, *try*."

> "What happens when you *try* to say your name... and you *try* to say... because it's *gone now* when you *try*."

If you're a geek for such things, you may remember the scene in *The Empire Strikes Back* where Yoda says to Luke Skywalker, "Try not. Do... or do not. There is no try."

Well, in hypnosis there most certainly *is* 'try', but only when creating what Yoda is aiming to help Luke avoid: we *want* Luke struggling to lift the X-wing so we'd say to him: "The harder you *try* the more it just sticks deeply... in the swamp". We evoke difficulty with '*try*' because trying is certainly *not* the same as succeeding.

Can

'Can' is a wonderful word for creating subtle suggestions. If you say to someone, "You can begin to feel the heaviness in your hand", you're not asserting that they definitely *will* feel that heaviness. You're merely implying that it's a *possibility*. In the realm of possibility, there's nothing solid to push back on because nothing has been stated as fact. The co-operator, in processing the suggestion, accepts at least the seed of the idea that their hand feels heavy.

The word 'can' is also useful when you're pacing. Imagine someone is gripping a playing card that you're going to stick between their finger and thumb. Instead of saying, "Feel your fingers gripping the card", say, "You can feel your fingers gripping the card as you continue to look at that point". Here you are using 'can' as a softener: by pacing this way we avoid sounding as if we're giving an order. This is always a good idea because, perhaps ironically, the more respect you show for a person's autonomy, the easier they are to influence. Conversely, push people and they tend to push back. By pacing your co-operator's reality in terms of possibility, you make the suggestion subtle and invitational, so 'can' is a useful way to take the 'push' out of suggestions while still seeding the ideas that you want to seed.

Allow

The word 'allow' is another useful option that can be paired with 'can' to keep us in the realm of leading rather than pushing:

> "You *can* allow yourself to *just relax* and *notice your breathing*."

The great thing about 'allow' is that it presupposes that something wants to happen (*happening*, rather than *doing*, is something of a hallmark of hypnotic phenomena). It's as if you're telling your co-operator they don't have to make it happen because it wants to happen anyway — they just have to take away resistance to it. 'Allow' is a nice, softening word that encapsulates the very essence of hypnosis — things happening outside of direct volition. You essentially want people to be focused in the moment and getting their analytical brain out of the way to *allow* these interesting phenomena to emerge simply through their *engagement*.

Now

One guiding principle I teach my students is 'get into versus get through'. When learning hypnosis, some people try to 'get through' the steps to reach the desired phenomenon. What they miss in doing this is that all phenomena happen *only in the present moment*. During a facilitation, we may play with time, tense, memory and future imagining but we are always working in the theatre of *now*.

'Now' is a wonderful word that pulls everything into *this moment*.

> "Just allow yourself to experience this freedom... *now*... because you can."

The word 'now' draws focus into the present, conveying presence and immediacy. Now... in hypnosis, we often play with the notions of past, present and future. When you're pre-engineering something, you say, "In a moment, but not yet", making it clear that whatever you're referring to has not yet happened. When you want something to happen immediately, use the word 'now'. You can sometimes use the past tense as well to set things up, like this:

> "As your hand *released* from the table, an interesting thing just *happened*... *now* you can notice that your mind is blank when you try to say your name."

This wording starts with the past tense ('released' and 'happened') but then pulls everything into the present with 'now' so as to deliver the next suggestion ('notice' followed by the 'blank mind' suggestion).

Here's an example of setting something up, pre-engineering and then collapsing back into the present moment when appropriate:

> "*In a moment, but not yet*, I'm going to ask you to open your eyes. *When you do*, an interesting thing will *have happened*. *When* you open your eyes, you *will* look, you will be unable to see me, you *will* look straight through me as if I were completely invisible. The clothes I'm wearing *will* be invisible. You *will* be unable to see me and anything that I'm wearing. So *go ahead*, allow your inner mind to *make that happen now*, you *can* open your eyes, you *can* hear my voice, but..."

In this example, I've put all the temporal language in italics so you can see how we move from the future tense to the present tense. You *first* give your co-operator the information they need to shape the experience. Having done this, and not before, you *then* trigger the experience itself with the phrase, "...make that happen now", coupled with the act of your co-operator opening their eyes.

Playing with time can be fun and useful but always remember that *all* hypnotic experience happens in the theatre of the *now*. This is why, of all the words pertaining to time, 'now' is on the magic words list. In general, if you're unsure where to go at any point in a facilitation, take your co-operator more fully into *this moment* and all it contains:

> Operator: "So... what is it that is happening right *now*?"

> Co-operator: *"I'm feeling more relaxed".*

> Operator: "And more relaxed... and noticing *this* relaxed... and relaxing more *now*... and letting this relaxed take you into new possibilities..."

Learn to fill 'the now' fully, richly, vibrantly and wonderfully and you will become a truly impactful hypnotic facilitator almost by default.

As If

This is more a magic phrase than a magic word, but one well worth bending the rules for. Sometimes it can even stretch out further to become the extra-powerful "almost as if". Here's a simple example:

> "It's *almost as if* you can float up... with a growing sense of comfort... all the way up above all the happenings of your everyday life..."

This little pattern has a lot of utility because it minimises resistance points while seeding ideas. In this example, had we bluntly requested, "Now float up above all the happenings of your everyday life", our co-operator might wonder how they should do that or even whether it's possible. 'Almost as if', on the other hand, applies no pressure whatsoever to make it happen, thus freeing the mind to simply follow the idea however it may.

 Here's another example:

> "As you continue to look at your hand, stuck out there in front of you on the table, and feel the table underneath your hand, it's almost as if your hand begins to... solidify."

You haven't said that the hand actually begins to solidify. You've simply said that it's *almost as if* the hand begins to solidify. In order to make sense of this, your co-operator has no choice but to go into their own mind and imagine what it would be like if their hand was indeed solidifying, then check in with what way their current experience of their hand is *almost* (but not quite) like that.

If you think about this in terms of the hypnotic loop, this pattern is a way to engage with the imagination element. As soon as your co-operator starts to imagine what you've mentioned (which they must to some degree in order to make sense of it), you can start to lead them further into it to make it more and more vivid.

Of course, the imagination (loop element 2) is going to start firing the physiology (loop element 3), which feeds forward into experience (loop element 4), which you can strategically feed back into beliefs (loop element 1). Hence 'as if' can be a strong means by which to enter and influence the hypnotic loop as a whole, enabling us to draw in new elements of our co-operator's imagination.

The Present Continuous Tense

We already spoke about how hypnosis happens 100% within the 'theatre of the now', and this is what makes the present continuous tense so profoundly useful to us in our work. Clearly, this isn't strictly a 'word', but I'm including it here because it surely is 'magic'!

You can recognise the present continuous tense by the suffix 'ing': 'experiencing', 'continuing', 'happening', 'becoming' and so on. These '—ing' words, known to grammarians as present participles, imply that something is happening and is going to continue happening. In hypnosis, we're always operating within the realm of ongoing experience so '—ing' words are very powerful:

> "And as you feel your body *relaxing*... and your mind *opening*... you might become curious... as to what is already *changing* now..."

The use of the present continuous tense makes descriptions much more vivid and 'alive'. To appreciate this, take a few moments to consider the word 'dance' (and do this like a wine expert would savour a fine wine - really connect into the word and what it evokes for you). Say it to yourself - 'dance'... what comes into your mind? Notice the qualities. Now clear your mind and consider instead the word 'dancing'. What does this evoke that is different from 'dance'? Take a few moments with it.

For most people, the word 'dancing' evokes a much more dynamic sense — images or feelings of something that's actually happening - whereas the word 'dance' evokes something more static. It is this tendency to bring things to life that makes the present continuous tense so useful to us as hypnotic facilitators, because richer experiences are always more impactful and meaningful. This is especially important if your aim is to use hypnosis to bring people to new ways of being and seeing that serve them better in their lives.

Congruence in Hypnotic Communication

The last idea I want to share in this section is congruence in communication.

Congruence in communication is said to occur when your nonverbal communication matches your verbal communication. In other words, your body language, gestures and facial expression all agree with and lend support to the actual words you say.

The only way to achieve this congruence is to completely believe in what you're doing and communicating. If you want to communicate that you are in charge and leading a process, but inside you're feeling afraid and unsure if it's going to work, there's a good chance that your doubt will leak through to the detriment of your facilitation (you will lack congruence in your delivery).

As the hypnotist, your role in the facilitation is to lead with clarity and certainty from a position of expertise and authority. This means you need to *feel* all of these things within yourself, so that the way you act and communicate is entirely congruent with the requirements of your role. When you deliver a suggestion, such as someone's hand sticking, the more fully you enter the reality that the hand can and will stick, the more effectively you will evoke that experience within your co-operator. Shape your own reality from the inside out and live into it with your heart, mind and entire being. This is the way to be absolutely and completely congruent with what you're doing.

Some hypnosis teachers suggest that you should aspire to be 'The Hypnotist'. This is their way of communicating this principle of congruence. The idea is that you shouldn't try to hypnotise people from an insecure base, but instead be The Hypnotist, with a capital 'T' and 'H'. Think of yourself in this way and believe in this role fully and completely. When you know, feel and believe that you're an excellent hypnotist, you come across to people in a much more powerful way. All your nonverbal communication automatically becomes congruent with everything you want to achieve, namely, being The Hypnotist and successfully achieving the facilitation of hypnosis.

This idea is sound in principle, but it can also put pressure on some people to adopt a character that they don't feel aligned with. If this is true for you, remember these words (attributed to Joseph Campbell): "you may not get to choose your role in life but you always get to choose how you play it." In the context of hypnosis, take this to mean that you get to be the kind of hypnotist you want to be. Remember, there is no consensus in the world of hypnosis (either academic or practical) as to what hypnosis actually is, which I'd attribute to the fact that it isn't a 'thing' so much as a practice or craft. As I already mentioned in our discussion on framing, this gives you very broad licence to make 'hypnosis' up to be anything that works for both you and your client. Similarly, you have licence to make yourself up to be the kind of hypnotist you want to be. Whatever kind of hypnotist this is, you will need to find your way to that certainty and authority in action. So how might you do this?

Clearly, the less experience you have, the more challenging this is likely to be. One approach is what you might call the 'method acting' approach: put yourself fully in the mindset of The Hypnotist. Close your eyes, do some visualisation, see yourself being The Hypnotist and doing hypnosis with competence and authority. Step inside this imagined picture of yourself so you can experience it from the inside. Feel what it's like to know that you can do hypnosis, you're doing a wonderful job, your co-operator is responsive and everything is working as it should. Know that you have this capability within you so that when you're doing hypnosis for real you adopt this role and achieve fully congruent communication. This approach can be useful but, for some, doubt and hesitancy can still seep.

It may help to recast yourself in your own mind as a curious explorer and experimenter. The aim of the game becomes to discover 'what happens when..?' What happens when this person places their hand down and focuses? What happens when they fully immerse themselves in the imagined experience of it sticking? What happened when it manifested as reality? What happened when it didn't (ask your co-operator to get useful feedback!)? What could you or they do differently next time to perhaps get a better result? The advantage of this approach is that you can *never* fail because you are making no claims to begin with. Your only aim is to engage with curiosity and discover whatever you discover. So long as you always gather usable feedback, you will always discover *something*, and any interesting phenomena that emerge can be taken as a bonus.

This is a good start, but the strange loop here is that one of the things you will want to experiment with on your way to certainty, is *certainty itself*. The more you are able to evoke the experience of certainty directly within yourself, the more it will be available to you as a tool for influence. One way of thinking about this is that you are 'method acting' certainty in order to strategically deploy it. Try this in small doses: for example, when you go for a name amnesia, at the moment you tell them that their name has gone, practise grounding yourself in the personal reality that it *absolutely has gone.*

Quick story. Once, during a workshop I was running in Melbourne, I set out to demonstrate a name amnesia only to have the co-operator bluntly state his name at the point of challenge. Because I had so fully distorted my own reality to believe his name was gone, without missing a beat I replied: "That's right, you can *try* and say it... t.. t.. *try* [pantomiming confusion and difficulty]" Interestingly, the amnesia then took beautifully! Afterwards, I sought feedback (experimenter frame!) to find out what had occurred for him. "You do know you said your name, right?", I asked. "Well, I thought I did", he replied, "but you made me doubt myself". That is the power of creating from the inside out. Going *fully* into the reality you wish to manifest *yourself.* (And if it doesn't, just smoothly pivot out of it and back into your experimenter frame.)

Congruence in communication is tremendously important if you want to be a successful hypnotist, but you may need to weave it together across time and experimentation. This is to be expected because hypnosis is a *craft*, and no craftsperson reaches the apex of their game overnight.

This brings us to the end of our discussions on verbal and nonverbal suggestion. In the next chapter, we'll be looking in to some tricks, tips and additional concepts for putting the cherries on top of your hypnosis cake.

5

ADDITIONAL CATALYSING CONCEPTS

5. Additional Catalysing Concepts

In this final section we will be looking at some additional concepts that will further enhance your hypnosis game. Were I a more structured thinker, these may have found places elsewhere in the book, but... well, here they are rounding things off.

The Hypnotist Leads

In Chapter 1 we unpacked the concept of the hypnotic partnership, which I strongly advocate as an orienting principle for successful hypnosis. I suggested that you avoid playing the role of a Svengali figure out to dominate someone's mind, and instead, respect this partnership (and your partner) as the foundation of the work.

That said, it is still imperative that, as the hypnotist, you are very much the leader of the dynamic — clearly in the driving seat of the process from beginning to end. We need to find a balance here: leading with absolute certainty whilst avoiding anything that might seem like coercion, manipulation or attempted domination. The aim here is to facilitate the process with respect, awareness and a light (but still authoritative) touch where necessary. We want to to encourage and to draw in, *not* cajole, push and pressure. Lead clearly with respect and sensitivity while *absolutely* avoiding hesitancy and doubt. This is what is required because if you act with any hesitation or let your co-operator lead, the whole house of cards comes falling down.

Throughout this book, I've held back from using too many stories or metaphors, preferring the conciseness of straightforward information and practical guidance.

However, I want to share an important point that I learned from the world of martial arts. I'm sharing this because you will no doubt encounter many different approaches as you further explore this fascinating craft, and I want to offer you this guidance on how they can inform each other.

Since my early 20s, I've studied what are called Chinese 'internal' martial arts. What defines these particular martial arts is that they generate power not through muscular strength but through fluid connectivity of the body. They are rooted in the philosophy of Taoism, from which we get the familiar Yin-Yang symbol.

The Taoist approach is all about dynamic interplay: looking for strength within weakness, dark within light, power within yielding and softness within hardness. It's about looking to work with the Yin-Yang relationships at play within all that you do.

There are three main internal martial arts: Tai Chi, Ba Gua Zhang and Xing Yi. In this section, I want to talk about two of them because, unlikely as it may seem, they serve as really useful metaphors.

Tai Chi Chuan might be described as the 'softest' of all the martial arts. It's about receiving and transforming incoming force rather than resisting or overcoming it. The fundamental spirit of Tai Chi is traditionally expressed using the metaphor of water. You can't attack water, because if you try to hit or strike it, the water just flows around your fist. At the same time, we all know that water can be extremely powerful. It can erode rocks or sweep people away.

In contrast, the fundamental spirit of Xing Yi is perhaps best expressed using the metaphor of a train. Someone trained in Xing Yi can be said to move *through* their opponent's space in a very hard, fast and direct way. They steam through, occupy the space and destroy everything in their path.

When I first started learning martial arts, my instructor said people are drawn to different disciplines based on their character. Tai Chi Chuan, he said, emphasises the Yin aspect, including notions of softness and yielding. Xing Yi emphasises the Yang aspect, a more dynamic and aggressive approach. This teacher's view was that if you have a Yin character, naturally yielding and not inclined to exercise power in a situation, it's a good idea to learn Xing Yi, which is very hard and direct, to help develop this other side to your character. On the other hand, if you're naturally a very Yang person, you're better off studying Tai Chi Chuan and learning to influence outcomes through subtler means.

What has all this got to do with hypnosis?

When I first developed an interest in hypnosis, I studied what's known as the Ericksonian approach. This is often called the *permissive* style of hypnosis as opposed to the *authoritarian* approach of classical hypnosis. As I became more aware of these different styles (permissive and authoritarian) I was reminded of the martial arts I've just mentioned.

Many people who are drawn to the Ericksonian approach are more Yin in character. They don't like to be direct with people or tell them what to do. They prefer to give people space to cultivate their own ideas and find their own directions. However, if you study Erickson in detail, you find that while his approach to hypnosis was very Yin, his character was actually quite Yang. He was a very clear leader, certain about what he wanted to achieve and where he wanted to go. He is reputed to have said, "I like to give people as much choice as possible in doing exactly what I want them to do." This really does sum up Erickson's approach. If you watch videos of his work, he has a Yang foundation underlying his very Yin/permissive approach, which is likely *why* he was so successful. However, a lot of permissive post-Ericksonian hypnotists don't have that Yang centre that Erickson had. They're out of balance (referred to as 'double-weighted' in Tai Chi parlance) and so they don't have the same effect or power.

Conversely, some hypnotists have a strong Yang character and practise very direct, authoritarian styles of hypnosis. Unfortunately, this 'double Yang' approach means they can often come across as pushy and bullying and, for this reason, tend to trigger push-back and resistance. They usually get round this by simply not working with people who show such resistance, which allows them to maintain an artificial illusion of efficacy whilst reducing the range of people they can effectively work with.

When learning hypnosis, consider your nature and what type of person you are. Think about which aspects of your character you might want to develop in order to grow as a person, hypnotist and influential communicator.

If you're generally more Yang in character, you already have tendencies to take charge and be the leader. To complement your Yang, develop the Yin side of your character. Focus on subtlety and leading people in a softer, more artful way. Study the communication techniques in this book and learn how to be indirect.

Alternatively, if you're a very Yin person, you will want to learn more about taking charge and being very direct and dynamic when it serves your purpose to do so. Remember the Yin-Yang symbol: within the white you have that little spot of darkness, and within the black you have that little spot of brightness. Within the Yang you have the Yin; within the Yin you have the Yang.

I appreciate this may sound somewhat esoteric, but I sincerely believe that all the very best hypnotists and influential communicators are adept at exploiting the interplay between hard and soft; authoritative direction and gentle leading and guiding. This is the key to flexible, adaptive and, ultimately, effective facilitation in hypnosis. It means always knowing when to hold and when to fold, when to lean in and when to lead out, when to stride and when to dance. Learn to fold these opposites into each other and great skill will come your way.

Flexibility and Utilisation

Hypnosis is, without question, a 'live art'. To borrow a maxim from the world of British special forces: nothing ever works without a plan, and no plan ever works. This most certainly applies in the realm of hypnotic facilitation — yes it serves us greatly to have clear outcomes and sound strategies for realising them, but once the game is on we need more than just that.

To be the very best hypnotists that we can be, we need to be fully present and fully 'switched on' in every moment of our hypnotic facilitations. We have to be alert and responsive, always attending to what's happening and ready to adjust our behaviour and communication as required by the unique dictates of every moment.

You'll note that throughout this book, whilst I have given plenty of examples of hypnotic languaging, I have completely avoided offering any 'hypnosis scripts'. Whilst it can be tempting for the beginner to seek out such scripts, they can in fact be damaging to both your development and the reputation of hypnosis in general. Why? Because they draw us away from understanding that hypnosis is about a living, breathing, interaction that unfolds moment by moment. The bottom line here is that *scripts don't facilitate hypnosis*, skilled hypnotic facilitators do. You will never become a truly successful hypnotist working from scripts (though you may get lucky from time to time). To attain proficiency in this craft, you need to work from a core understanding of the principles and psychological factors involved, constantly evaluating the situation and adjusting your behaviour accordingly. This is where you want to be thinking in terms of flexibility and utilisation — to learn to create with whatever comes up.

I want to share a model from the world of cybernetics (the study of control systems) that greatly helped me when I started out as a hypnotist. It's called the TOTE model: 'Test Operate Test Exit'. It provides a template for creating outcomes within the context of changing situational conditions. The essence of a TOTE loop is this:

First you get a clear outcome in mind, then you simply take an action (*operate*) to move you towards this goal. Next you evaluate this action (*test*): did it realise your outcome, move you closer to it, do nothing or move you further from it? If it realised the outcome, you can *exit*. If not, you need to take a *different* action (*operate*) then test again. You continue to test and operate until you attain your outcome, at which point you exit.

To illustrate this, imagine you want to steer a boat under a narrow bridge (the term 'cybernetics' is derived from the Greek 'kubernētēs' meaning the 'steersman' of a boat or ship). The outcome is simply to pass under the bridge without collision. As you approach the bridge, you would visually *test* to see that you were on course. If so, the only operation required is to continue moving forward. If you are heading too far to the left, the *operation* would be to steer to the right. From here you would continue with tests and operations until you finally pass under the bridge (or crash into it if the appropriate operations were not made).

I share this model because successful hypnosis relies on running effective TOTE loops. At any given moment, you want to know what you are trying to achieve. You also know how to test whether your facilitation is on course, your co-operator is showing green flag behaviours, there are signs of the loop manifesting and so on. Are you where you want to be? Good — you can progress with the session. If not, you need to take action, apply a correction, make an adjustment and get things back on track. You can only do this if you take a *flexible* approach to hypnosis. This means being able to make use of whatever happens during a hypnotic interaction, even if it's not what you intended, to get things heading once more in a useful direction. To do this we most certainly need principles, strategies and tactics to inform our operations, along with the skills and mindset to implement them, *but never scripts.*

Consider this hypothetical example. Imagine you are working with a co-operator to create an experience of her hand being stuck to her head. You have set the loop and had plenty of green flags so you go to challenge: "What happens when you try and un*stick* that hand?" And she slowly but tentatively lifts the hand! So what do you do?

The answer is *utilisation*: you create with what you have!

What have you got here? Slow tentative lifting is not the same as just shrugging and flicking the bird at you. I have had this kind of response occur many times and my counter-response is always the same: pace it and lead with a question!

Operator: "And it lifts... slowly... it lifts... (note here 'it lifts' not 'you lift it' — keep it in the realm of *happening* not *doing*)... and what is it like... when it lifts slowly like that?"

Co-operator: "It's really stiff."

And we have the lead we need!

Operator: "And it's really stiff... and notice the stiffness... growing..."

So we are still working the loop! If we had been working from a script but with no understanding, we'd have had little choice but to give up, thinking "it hasn't worked". Alternatively, you can *utilise* what has happened. We can think of utilisation as the act of making use of something in a creative way, that leads us towards creative outcomes. I want to emphasise this — *creative outcomes*. This does *not* necessarily mean the outcome you originally had in mind, only an outcome that serves (or can be framed as serving) broader aims.

So let's go back to our 'hand stuck to head' example. Let's imagine a 'worst case scenario' (one I have *never* encountered, by the way) — our co-operator has been playing us the whole time and has faked all the green flags just to set us up for a fall. So we issue the challenge ("What happens when you try and un*stick* that hand?") and they *do* flick us the bird whilst laughing like Nelson from 'The Simpsons'. How do we utilise this?

Firstly, we *don't* buy their 'me versus you' framing (we always want to be the one deploying and managing the frames, not the one reacting to them). Instead we simply state, "That's right (*validating* their action) because *you* are in complete control and *this* is not mind control... and there is no rule that says you have to have a different kind of experience here... the choice *is* yours... but you most certainly *can*." So here we utilise the happening in the service of reinforcing their autonomy. I pointed out this paradox before: the more you sincerely respect a person's autonomy, the more open they become to influence.

We are still in the game. Still in the position of leadership. Still laying the frames (rather than reacting to theirs). Still working strategically. Essentially, we are *still hypnotising*!

In my view, this is where the work gets really deep and interesting, and starts to teach us true lessons for life. The point here that is when you learn to utilise and think in terms of dynamic TOTES, your work can *never fail* (although you are free to creatively shift your outcomes and frames to accommodate the situation).

All that said, I do not wish to give the impression that utilisation is all about avoiding disaster. It can equally be about steering the process more successfully or augmenting the quality of the experience you are facilitating. Suppose, for example, you are in the early phase of facilitating hypnotic focus with your co-operator and you become aware that they seem to be being distracted by some background noise. You might choose to draw the sounds into the loop to prevent them from drawing your co-operator out:

> "Notice how the sounds... around... are part of *this* experience... sounds moving through and focusing you... into that point on the tip of your finger... and all the sounds focus into that point too."

Legendary hypno-psychiatrist Milton Erickson was known to be a true master of utilisation and I highly recommend that you study his work if you wish to master the craft of hypnosis. Here is one of many stories that illustrate his artistry.

Erickson was running a workshop on hypnosis for some physicians and was some way into his presentation when one of the audience stood up and said, "I'm sorry, Doctor Erickson, but this is complete and absolute nonsense. There is absolutely no way that you could get me into trance."

Erickson replied, "That's right, I couldn't get you into trance... any more than you would be able to step out into the aisle."

With some indignation, the challenging physician countered with words and action: "Of course I can step out into the aisle!" and did just so to prove it.

Erickson followed, "That's right, you *can* step out into the aisle but you can't *take four steps towards the stage*".

Incredulous still, and determined to prove Erickson wrong, the admant sceptic replied: "Of course I can take four steps towards the stage." And so he demonstrated.

Erickson: "That's right... of course you can take four steps forward towards the stage. But you can't *step up on to the stage*". Rising to the challenge, the sceptic stepped up onto the stage.

Erickson: "That's right... of course you can step up onto the stage. But you can't *sit down* in that chair and go *deeply into trance*." The man looked at the chair in confusion. "That's right..." continued Erickson. To the surprise and amusement of the audience, the challenger sat down in the chair and closed his eyes.

I don't know (or much care) whether this story is true or not but it certainly captures something of Erickson's spirit while also beautifully illustrating the principle of utilisation. In this case it was the audience member's inclination to be defiant that Erickson utilised. He set up a loop founded in the dynamics of challenge that drew the sceptic on to the stage, leading him to sit in the chair and go into trance (or at least close his eyes and assume a congruent posture).

Here's another example taken from a recording of a seminar by hypnotist David Caloff.

Caloff: "How do you feel at the moment?"

Volunteer: "Fine."

"So you're not in any trance or anything at the moment?"

"No."

"Are you sure?"

"Yes, I'm sure."

"Are you really sure?"

"Yes, I'm really sure."

"Are you sure enough... to allow an element of doubt to creep in?"

Isn't this a neat little binding pattern? (It certainly got the audience giggling!).

Volunteer: "No, no, I am sure."

Caloff: "How about your hand, is your hand sure?"

This is an beautiful hypnotic question. If the volunteer says, "No, my hand's not sure", then he is to some extent undermining his position of being sure. Then again, if he says his hand is sure, he is buying into the dissociating idea that his hand has a will separate from his own.

Volunteer: "Yes, yes, yes."

Caloff: "How about your eyes, are your eyes sure?"

"Yes."

"As sure as when you look at me, you'll be unable to say your name now. Look at me."

At this point in the recording, the volunteer looks at Caloff, and apparently finds just that!

This is an absolutely beautiful piece of utilisation (one of my all time favourites, hence my sharing of it here): taking what's happening in the moment and completely turning it around. (There's a lot of great material in David Caloff's 'Hypnotic Techniques' audio series, which I strongly recommend.)

To sum up, flexibility and the ability to create with whatever comes up is the true backbone of all great hypnotic work, and the principle of utilisation is the platform upon which such skill is built. Master this craft and it will serve you in life *way beyond* the narrow context of formal hypnotic facilitation. Whatever happens, take it, own it and create forward with it.

Curiosity Framing

One frame that I regularly deploy during my hypnotic facilitation work is the *curiosity frame*. This is *not* a major pre-frame that provides a 'big because'; more a frame that I deploy as I go to aid co-operator engagement with the work. Essentially, when my co-operator hypothetically wonders, "What is it that is going on here?", I want at least part of the answer to be in the realm of, "A curious and fascinating experience". Fundamentally, I want them to perceive what's happening as a fascinating experience that stimulates their curiosity. But, *why* do I want this?

Essentially, because the cognitive process/state of curiosity is tremendously useful to us in shaping appropriate engagement. Curiosity 'pulls people in' and has them attend more closely as well as taking them out of critical thinking. It is a state that is mutually exclusive with fearfulness and the corresponding desire to control. Initially, someone may come to the game believing that hypnosis means being 'out of control' and that they may be vulnerable in some way during the process. Instead of trying to *convince* them that their fears are unfounded (which would be unlikely to work), I prefer instead to lead them clearly into the kind of experience that I want them to have: one of curiosity and fascination.

A very powerful way to establish any frame is to act and behave *as if* the frame were true — come from the reality that you wish to evoke! To set yourself on the path with this regarding the curiosity frame, answer for yourself this question: "How would I *feel* and *behave* if hypnosis was *absolutely fascinating* and *only* led people to have *really interesting* experiences they felt *intensely curious* about?"

I invite you to really 'connect in' to this in rich detail; to imagine it so vividly that you lose yourself in the daydream of it. Really *experience the curiosity* and fascination yourself. In NLP this is called the 'go there first principle': if you want someone to experience an attitude or state *go there yourself first*. So, if you want someone to experience curiosity and fascination, go there first.

If you watch me facilitating hypnosis, you will often see places where I explicitly display curiosity, often through saying things like:

> "You know it's an *interesting* thing... something *really curious* has just happened. Now what's that like, when you try to lift your hand and you find it sticks even more now; it's *a weird thing*, isn't it?"

All of this is accompanied by nonverbal indications of curiosity (you'll have to imagine how they may look and sound). The very fact that I *look* and *sound* curious about what's happening is what establishes the curiosity frame first and foremost — the words come second! This is a highly effective way to keep people out of fear and so helps to prevent them retreating from the process. They become just as fascinated and absorbed in the process as I am.

I strongly advocate that you use curiosity framing in your own work and ensure that you deploy it from the inside out — *go there first!* If you want people to be curious, be curious! Be the resonator so that they may resonate.

Contrast Convincers

Never waste an opportunity to add in any little bit of business to your work that might ratify for your co-operator that something unusual is happening. The *contrast convincer* is one such bit. To see how this works, let's say you've facilitated an arm lock experience for your co-operator and you say:

> "...go ahead... try to bend that arm, find it's locked now..."

Your co-operator tries to bend their arm and struggles to do so. Now for the contrast convincer:

"You can move that other arm easily, can't you?"
(they proceed to move the other arm easily).

As they demonstrate to themselves that they can move the other arm easily, the contrast between one arm and the other strongly reinforces the shift in reality you have generated. This is a neat little ratifier because you are not trying to convince your co-operator in any way, only letting them convince *themselves*. This is a nice little piece, quick and easy to use, so well worth making use of where you can.

Reality Reports in the Long Game

In the section on 'Managing Hypnotic Loops', we looked at the idea of eliciting *reality reports*: prompting your co-operator to describe something of the experience they are having. I want to add something to this regarding the long-term effects of eliciting and utilising reality reports and how to leverage those effects in your favour.

As we have seen, when you elicit reality reports, you are harnessing the principles of commitment and consistency. Your co-operator has verbally committed to what's being produced by the loop and will therefore likely behave in a consistent manner, which further reinforces the loop. However, it's important to realise that this consistency will likely stay in place *long after the hypnotic session is over*.

Here's a problem that will be familiar to many hypnotists. Let's say you've demonstrated some of the effects of hypnosis with someone, it seems to go well, their reality shifts and then it shifts back again. Afterwards, the co-operator says:

> "Yeah, that was interesting, but I could have lifted my hand / remembered my name if I'd really wanted to though."

This isn't necessarily a problem (utilise the answer to create forward!), but when you elicit reality reports, and get commitment and consistency in the moment, this kind of thing just tends not to happen anymore because the consistency produced endures beyond the close of the final loop. In short, people generally won't subsequently contradict what they committed to in the moment. To be clear, this is not a superficial effect: they will make themselves congruent from the inside out.

Remember, as a hypnotist you are a shaper of perceived reality. This goes beyond the session, into the world and people's broader perceptions of who you are and what you do. People will take that consistency into their conversations with others and become ambassadors for the efficacy of your work. Eliciting and utilising reality reports helps to create them as such 'ambassadors'.

Narration of Action

Narration of action is a form of pacing, but instead of serving to set up for leading, it is undertaken to create a sense of *ongoing flow*. You use it whenever you do something as part of the facilitation that, while peripheral to your suggestion work, is necessary and so needs to be brought into the linguistic flow.

For example, suppose you're working with a co-operator who is currently experiencing a stiff, rigid arm. Next, you want to stick their hand to their head. To do this, you need to move their arm. Instead of pausing while you perform this action, narrate what you are doing to bring this action into the flow of your ongoing communication:

> "Now as I touch you on the elbow [touch the elbow], you can feel that softening now, I'm going to take you by the wrist and the arm [take the wrist and arm], you feel that softening just letting go [gently shaking it loose], that's right, and as that hand touches the head now [placing the hand firmly on the head] locking solidly in place."

You are *narrating* the action in order to *pace* the action.

If you don't pace the action in this way (for example just grabbing the arm and abruptly moving it), your co-operator might be popped out of the experience as they wonder what's going on. This can lead to their critical faculty coming back into play in a way that would be detrimental to the work.

Simply by narrating the action, you can keep everything that you're doing within the smooth flow of the facilitation.

Managing Eye Movement

Managing eye movement is a powerful way to influence where your co-operator can and cannot easily go within their mind and attention. Anyone who has studied NLP to any degree will have been exposed to the notion of *eye accessing* and eye accessing *cues*. The idea is that people

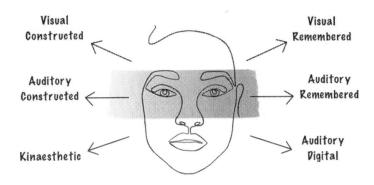

Visual Constructed

Visual Remembered

Auditory Constructed

Auditory Remembered

Kinaesthetic

Auditory Digital

tend to move their eyes in different ways depending on whether they're *retrieving* or *constructing* information, as well as on whether it's visual information or auditory information and so on. As part of their NLP practitioner training, students practise asking people questions and paying attention to their eye movements to get a sense of the kind of information they are retrieving.

There is some controversy around NLP eye accessing cues with some claiming the whole notion has been 'scientifically debunked'. In fact, what was 'debunked' was a claim (that these cues could indicate lying) that was never actually made by the originators of the idea. Personally, I am not convinced as to the reliability of the classic eye accessing cues map. However, let me share a story.

I recall an occasion back in my NLP trainer days when one of the trainees decided as a challenge to *not* move her eyes when answering questions designed to elicit eye-accessing responses. The interesting thing was not that she was successful, but that she became completely unable to answer any of the questions so long as she kept her eyes in a fixed, forward position. These were simple questions like, "What did you have for breakfast?" or, "What's your favourite song?". I offer this example not to claim that this would happen in this exact way for everyone, but to illustrate that there does indeed seem to be some relationship between eye movement and our ability to access information from memory. So how can we use this?

If you watch me demonstrating the elicitation of name amnesia with a person you will see that, at the point of challenge, I work to limit their eye-accessing, telling them to 'look at me' while gesturing to my own eyes. In doing this, I'm not trying to 'mesmerise' them in the classical manner. It is simply a way of inhibiting their eye-accessing when they go to retrieve their name. Even if this adds only a few more percentage points of confusion or difficulty to their processing at this point, it can add significantly to the success of the effect. While I don't think this is essential to achieve name amnesia, I think it can be a powerful addition to whatever process you normally use.

Another way in which we, as hypnotists, manage eye movement is by simple fixation of attention — directing our co-operators to focus on a point on their hand or a mark on a wall. Our aim here is to minimise internal dialogue through limiting the corresponding eye accessing, and so 'quieten the mind'.

Eye accessing cues vary tremendously from one person to the next. Some people seem to need to move their eyes a lot in order to access memories while others can get by with very little eye movement. Nonetheless, I think that through suitably managing your co-operator's eye movements, you do significantly inhibit their ability to play their own mental 'games', thus leaving them more receptive to the new experiences you are leading them into.

Managing Internal Dialogue

People who have a lot of internal dialogue going on tend to be a little bit more challenging to work with hypnotically. This is partly because internal dialogue is the primary medium for critical thinking and partly because commentary on experience tends to step people back from the experience rather than immerse them in it.

(Incidentally, although 'internal monologue' might seem a more apt term, given that there is technically only one person involved, 'internal dialogue' has become the accepted usage. Although the voice may be singular, when it comes to critical thinking the form is often dialectical.)

This leads to an interesting question: what can you do to reduce or quieten someone's internal dialogue?

We have already discussed the role of limiting eye accessing in this capacity, and this is why eye fixation is the central part of our process for establishing hypnotic focus. Another option is to give our co-operator's internal dialogue something to do that is aligned with the outcomes we seek. For example, when I facilitate the card stick, I might instruct my co-operator to mentally repeat the words, "I am going to drop this," over and over in a loop. This occupies their internal dialogue and keeps it busy which, in turn, helps to diminish their critical faculty (note that the autosuggestion presupposes that it has not yet been dropped — this is the moment I want to suspend them in, to keep them from dropping it).

You can also give simple suggestions to banish the person's internal dialogue! I got this idea from watching the work of my friend and colleague Ravi Meyer. Ravi often weaves the suggestion, "Your thoughts are gone" into the flow of things when suggesting something particularly outlandish.

I really like this simple idea and have often made good use of it; clear out that default thinking to create space for the new thoughts you are suggesting. I tend to use this most when attempting the more dramatic phenomena that I feel might be more likely to trigger the critical faculty. Suppose I'm facilitating the experience of me being invisible. I might give the pre-engineering suggestions for my invisibility interspersed with the statement, "Your thoughts are gone."

> "When you open your eyes, you'll see right through me... your thoughts are gone, just gone completely... You'll see right trough me like I'm invisible... as your thoughts are gone now... invisible though you'll continue to hear my voice..."

I sometimes use a variant of this when I'm working with someone who has shown themselves to be a particularly critical or analytical thinker. In this case, I invite them to analyse the words themselves, like this:

> "And as you do that, I'd like you to think about the words 'your thoughts are gone' and what they might mean to you... now as you feel your feet inside your shoes... and you're breathing comfortably... and 'your thoughts are gone' are words that you can make sense of now... you continue to look... you continue to feel that," and so on and so forth.

As well as creating a little bit of confusion and mental overload, I'm explicitly inviting my analytical co-operator to analyse the words "your thoughts are gone". This works on a couple of levels. First, I am taking up their internal dialogue channel with activity of my choosing. Secondly, I'm creating a reason to repeat the embedded suggestion 'your thoughts are gone'.

If you ever get the chance to see Ravi Meyer doing his stuff, do take it! He's well worth seeing and learning from.

Misdirection and Overload

Here are two more ways to deal with a very analytical or critical attitude: misdirection and overload.

Sometimes, you may be giving good, well structured suggestions to your co-operator but as soon as they consciously catch themselves starting to respond they pop themselves out of it. One way around this is to to distract their conscious attention at strategic moments. Suppose, for example, you're demonstrating 'magnetic hands' (hands held out in front, pulling together as if by magnetic force) but this problem of conscious disruption means your co-operator is getting in their own way. In this situation, you might continue to give the magnetic hands suggestion but, at the same time, distract the co-operator's conscious attention:

> "So those hands can just continue to float out there in front of you... as you feel that sense they're going to come together in a moment and they're already starting to move... although you may not yet *feel them moving* they can move together... as you become aware of your feet... and you're breathing now... comfortably... as you continue to breathe you can just forget... this moment...."

So here you are creating distraction through drawing attention to the feet and the breathing, and thus giving the space for the previous suggestions to do their work unhindered. The trick here is to have given sufficient suggestions *before* you start distracting the co-operator. I strongly recommend you give this a go if you sense that your co-operator is unintentionally disrupting the process through conscious awareness (this is different from consciously and intentionally disrupting the process, which would be a problem of buy in). This doesn't always work but it does work reasonably often and it costs you nothing to deploy.

Another way to counteract an unhelpful critical faculty is to *overload* your co-operator's mind. One way you might do this is by means of *ambiguous touch*. This is where you make light but unusual touches to your co-operator's arms, shoulders or back. (Use your common sense as regards touching people - pre-announce the touch, avoid sensitive areas, pay attention to feedback and stop if they are pulling away or stiffening up.) If you're setting up an arm catalepsy, for example, these random touches are a way to overload their kinaesthetic processing channel. At the same time, you'd be pacing their visual and auditory experiences and leading them in the direction of setting up the desired hypnotic loop, the catalepsy that you want. The co-operator here has too much information to deal with consciously, making it much more difficult for them to play their own game.

There are all kinds of ways to achieve overload but the basic idea is to pace across the co-operator's visual, auditory and kinaesthetic channels and fill them with as much information as possible to create *noise*, through which you feed the *signal* of your loop suggestions.

Coaching Engagement

This is a simple but phenomenally powerful idea that is overlooked by the vast majority of hypnotists: simply coaching the engagement that you want!

If you went for golf lessons and you were holding the club poorly, you might expect that the instructor would give you some basic coaching on it: "OK, drop your shoulders a little and move your lower hand up to meet your other hand... let the grip be softer." This golf coach has a clear idea of how things need to be, and so can directly coach adjustments. Hypnotists can do this too. Does your co-operator look like they're focused? If not, coach adjustments until they look right to you. Are they frowning with their head cocked to one side in critical evaluation? Coach that frown away and get that head upright, relaxed and centralised. Have they revealed critical thinking during a reality report elicitation? Coach them to choose to let it go for a time and instead become fully absorbed.

Let me give a specific example. Let's say you are at the front end of setting up the initial loop and are giving your co-operator some simple instructions. You find they are verbally interjecting a lot with, "Uh huh, okay, yeah, right..." and so on. You don't want them doing this because it's clearly a part of their 'game' which you want them to drop, in order to play a new one. Here you simply coach: "You don't have to say anything." In context, it might sound like this:

> "As you continue to look at your hand ["uh huh"]...
> you don't have to say anything here, only focus...
> and notice your breathing... and follow the sound of
> my voice into this experience."

Directly coaching the engagement you want is a simple yet phenomenally useful way to increase the efficacy of your work. I think that many hypnotists overlook it because they see it as somehow cheating to plainly ask their co-operator for what they want rather than attain it all by clever suggestion. To me, there is no cheating in hypnosis, only means and ends, and coaching engagement is a useful means indeed.

Final Tips

Before drawing this book to a close, there are a few final tips I'd like to share with you.

Laughter

One of the best green flags you can get when a phenomenon is taking is the laughter of surprise. Let's say you have someone in a hypnotic loop. If you challenge them and they laugh as they get bound in the challenge, it shows they're surprised by what's happening.

When we see surprise, we know that what our co-operator is experiencing *must have* only just popped into consciousness in that moment (otherwise it wouldn't be a surprise!). The experienced phenomenon *is* 'mind made', but that it has only just appeared in consciousness tells us with clarity that the making was done significantly outside of consciousness. This, of course, is exactly what we are looking for.

Respect and Encouragement

When I first learned formal hypnosis, many sources advocated flattering the clients throughout the work. As a strategy, the idea is simple - the more praise you give your 'subject', the more 'compliant' they will be. For example, you might tell them they have a powerful inner mind or praise their intelligence and imagination. The principle behind this is sound, but in practise it can backfire as it can easily come across as insincere or sycophantic.

Instead, I would advocate that you cultivate genuine respect for your co-operator's capacities. Instead of just telling them they have a powerful inner mind, *know it to be true!* (People *do* have powerful minds — their capacity to shift their own reality and generate new behaviours is almost limitless in range if not scope.)

This is less about what you *do* and more about what you *see* and how you acknowledge it to your clients and co-operators. To develop this, start making it a habit to seek out people's strengths. Think of everyone you know — what can you find to admire about them? Cultivate the ability to truly wonder at small things rather than ignoring them, dismissing them or taking them for granted.

The more you respect and appreciate the people you work with, the more you are able to see and value their qualities and the more you can allow this to shine through naturally, in an unforced way. On a fundamental level it will change your whole way of being with them, which is no small thing. If this feels too esoteric for you, put it on the back-burner until such time as it doesn't... at which point you'll find that it makes a huge difference for you in your hypnotic facilitation work as well as your broader experience in life.

Focusing

I want to share a few extra focusing tips here. When setting up a point of focus, it is useful to do so in a way that is going to be most congruent with the first experience you intend to evoke. For example, if you want the first loop to be one of letting go and drifting into a pleasant mental journey, you might invite your co-operator to focus on a point then say something like:

> "And as you focus... on that point... you can allow yourself to become fully absorbed in... in this moment ."

Here the term 'fully absorbed' is chosen for its metaphorical richness; it is evocative in encouraging a 'drawing in' to the experience (remember, hypnotic language works more like poetry than it does dry, technical prose). You are encouraging them to become *fully absorbed* in the moment and in all that is happening within it. There is nothing abrupt about absorption, so it is congruent with the more relaxed, 'spacey' feel we're looking to create.

Alternatively, you might want to lock someones fingers tightly to a business card. This phenomenon has a very different quality to it so you will want to facilitate the focusing with that quality in mind. Here I might say:

> "Pick a point on that card that you can focus on *intently*... focus on *intently* as you feel the card between the fingers... the fingers *gripping* the card..."

The operative word is 'intently'. This has a very different 'energy' to it — indeed, much more intent! (I will often alternate between 'intently' and 'intensely' as I weave my suggestions in this context).

Also, be aware that the tonality, rhythm and rate of speech will be different in both examples, as will other aspects of nonverbal communication.

Another idea on focus that can be useful comes to us from 19th century hypnosis pioneer James Braid. Braid actually coined the term 'hypnotism', and initially believed it to consist in a special state of mind. Later in his career (as his understanding developed) he proposed that his original term should be replaced with a new term: 'monoideism'. Braid considered this a better fit, as it had become apparent to him that the various 'hypnotic phenomena' were not a product of a special state, but of the mind becoming tightly wrapped around a single idea (it goes without saying that his renaming didn't catch on). We can, however, take this idea of monoideism and use it to inform our focusing of people into experiences:

"Notice your hands wanting to pull together... don't make it happen and don't stop it from happening, just allow your mind to become wrapped around that single idea *now*... hands coming together, fully and completely... in your mind now..."

Now Make It Real

Finally, I want to intentionally repeat a point I've already made at the front of this book. If you want to become a good hypnotist, you will need to do a lot more than just read. Go into the world and practise, practise and practise some more. Find as many different people to practise, explore and experiment with as you possibly can. Regard any failure as merely feedback so take it in your stride. In short:

Do the work to make it real.

It has been said by some that to become proficient in any field you need to build up 10,000 hours of experience. This notion, based on the research of psychologist K. Anders Ericsson, is controversial when stated this simply but it can serve as a useful guide. The basic message is 'put the time in'. Get out there, get practising and even if you can't clock up 10,000 hours at least practise enough to develop your expertise and become an excellent hypnotist.

On the flip-side, if you find the idea of 10,000 hours rather daunting, author and business coach Josh Kaufman has noted that just twenty hours of solid practice can lead to *significant skill development* for beginners. You might like to check out his TedX Talk, 'The First 20 Hours: How To Learn Anything', to see what he achieved in just twenty hours spent learning the ukulele from scratch. Whichever view you take, perhaps the simple rule shared with me by my old coaching mentor Steve Chandler says it best:

Time spent developing your skills is the only way to develop your skills.

One thing that can really help is to set up a hypnosis practise group. It's easy to do and you can hire a hall if you haven't got enough space in your home. Put the word out, advertise, promote it online and meet up with like-minded individuals who are just as fascinated by hypnosis as you are. As well as practising with one another, you can go out into the street, into pubs, bars and coffee shops and practise hypnosis at every opportunity. If you're nervous about practising hypnosis, this is possibly all the more reason to get outside of your comfort zone and do it. This really is the single most important tip in this whole book, so please do take it on board.

If you find yourself living nowhere near others who might want to practise, get online and find like-minded people (visit HypnosisWithoutTrance.com for more help with that) - there is much you can do via Skype or Zoom!

So here we are at the end of 'Hypnosis Without Trance: How Hypnosis Really Works'. It is my sincerest wish that you take this material into the real world and start exploring; that you make wonderful things happen for you and for everyone you work with.

Thank you for buying this book and reading it all the way through, and I hope that at some point I get to meet you in person and hear your stories of exploration with Hypnosis Without Trance.

About James Tripp

James Tripp is an internationally recognised and respected developmental coach and teacher of hypnosis and influential communication.

Coming from a diverse background including philosophy, music, martial arts, movement culture and NLP, James has worked professionally as a hypnosis-based change agent since 2006, having previously worked as a manual therapist and close-up magician.

As the developer of the critically acclaimed Hypnosis Without Trance approach to hypnotic facilitation, James has taught workshops internationally and his UK workshops also typically draw students from around the world.

You can find out more about James and his work in hypnosis at HypnosisWithoutTrance.com, and his work in personal resourcing at JamesTripp.online. You can also join the 21k strong community of subscribers to his YouTube channel, where you can browse the hypnosis demonstration (and beyond) playlists and ask questions via the comments sections.

- - -

This material has taught me more about Hypnosis than my previous 20 years in Psychology and 4 years as a practicing Hypnotherapist [and] should be a standard requirement for ANY Hypnotist wanting to bring about real change work...If you don't learn this stuff you will be left behind!

Michael Skirving – DNLP, DHyp, LAPHP West Mids

Well, I have finished (more than once) [your] courses. Absolutely brilliant. Explained so that even I can understand it. Good stuff. Thanks.

J. Crit Harley – , MD, C.Ht., USA

My approach to the art is in a wonderful phase of evolution and a lot of it is due to Hypnosis Without Trance.

Andy Brady – Hypnotherapist, Ireland

You explain and demonstrate practical applications better than any one else I have ever studied.

Debbie Pitzel – Regina, Saskatchewan, Canada

I believe you are an important hub in the wheel that is turning hypnosis into wider acceptance and utilization as we advance further in our understanding of what hypnosis is; and just as importantly, what it is not!

Ron Franks – Hypnotist, Hamilton, NJ, United States

please visit

www.hypnosiswithouttrance.com

for hypnosis training and resources

Printed in Great Britain
by Amazon